Carleton Renaissance Plays in Translation

General Editors: Donald Beecher, Massimo Ciavolella

Editorial Advisors: H. Peter Clive, Gordon J. Wood,
J. Douglas Campbell, Leonard G. Sbrocchi, Mark Phillips

Carleton Renaissance Plays in Translation offer the student, scholar, and general reader a selection of sixteenth-century masterpieces in modern English translations, most of them for the first time. The texts have been chosen for their intrinsic merits and for their importance in the history of the development of the theatre. Each volume contains a critical and interpretive introduction intended to increase the enjoyment and understanding of the text. Reading notes illuminate particular references, allusions, and topical details. The comedies chosen as the first texts have fast-moving plots filled with intrigues. The characters, though cast in the stock patterns of the genre, are witty and amusing portraits reflecting Renaissance social customs and pretensions. Not only are these plays among the most celebrated of their own epoch, but they directly influenced the development of comic opera and theatre throughout Europe in subsequent centuries.

In print:

Odet de Turnèbe, **Satisfaction All Around (Les Contens)**
Translated with an Introduction and Notes by Donald Beecher

Annibal Caro, **The Scruffy Scoundrels** (Gli Straccioni)
Translated with an Introduction and Notes by Massimo
Ciavolella and Donald Beecher

In preparation:

Giovan Maria Cecchi, **The Owl** (L'Assiuolo)
Translated with an Introduction and Notes by Konrad
Eisenbichler

Jean de La Taille, **The Rivals** (Les Corrivaus)
Translated with an Introduction and Notes by H.P. Clive

Lope de Vega y Carpio, **The King and the Farmer** (El Villano
en su Rincón)
Translated with an Introduction and Notes by Adolfo Lozano
and Michael Thompson

Alessandro Piccolomini, **Alessandro**
Translated with an Introduction and Notes by Rita
Belladonna

Jacques Grévin, **Taken by Surprise** (Les Esbahis)
Translated with an Introduction and Notes by Leanore
Lieblein and Russell McGillivray

Carleton Renaissance Plays in Translation

Annibal Caro
THE SCRUFFY SCOUNDRELS
(Gli Straccioni)

Translated with an Introduction and Notes by
Massimo Ciavolella
and
Donald Beecher

Wilfrid Laurier University Press

1980

Canadian Cataloguing in Publication Data

Caro, Annibal, 1507-1566.
The Scruffy Scoundrels

(Carleton Renaissance plays in translation
ISSN 0704-4569) A play.

Translation of: Gli Straccioni
Bibliographies: p.
ISBN 0-88920-103-X [pbk] I. Title   II. Series

PQ 4617.C4S8713   852′.4   C81-094217-8

Copyright © 1981, Carleton University Renaissance
Centre & Wilfrid Laurier University Press
Waterloo, Ontario, Canada N2L 3C5

80   81   82   3   2   1

Typesetting and lay-out by
PGTA Professional Graphics Translation and Advertising Limited

Acknowledgements

The final version of this play has profited considerably from the many helpful comments and insights we received along the way from several of our colleagues at Carleton University. We wish to express here our thanks to Mark Phillips and Douglas Campbell for their invaluable observations concerning matters of tone and diction in the translation, to Gordon Wood, Raymond Morrison and Douglas Campbell for their thoughtful readings of the Introduction which rescued us from numerous inaccuracies and infelicities, and to Michael Thompson for his help with the reading of the galley proofs.

An honourable mention is more than merited by Irene Sanna who so patiently prepared typewritten versions of the script in all its various phases.

Finally, we wish to acknowledge our gratefulness to Carl Amberg, Dean of Graduate Studies and Research, and to Naomi Giffiths, Dean of Arts, for the publication grant needed to see this second title in our series through the press.

Introduction

Life

Annibal Caro was born June 19, 1507 in Civitanova Marche, a small town overlooking the Adriatic Sea, to Giambattista *aromatarius*, a well-to-do grocer. At the age of eighteen he set out for Florence, still one of the main centres of European intellectual life, to further his education and to make his fortune. There his intelligence and wit led to early renown. Through his friendship with Benedetto Varchi, a fellow student and a Florentine, he was admitted into the household of Monsignor Giovanni Gaddi, Clerk of the Apostolic Chamber, first as tutor of the Monsignor's nephew Lorenzo Lenzi, and then as Gaddi's own private secretary. Soon after, he found himself in Rome where his position enabled him to come into close contact with the entourage of the Farnese Pope, Paul III, and with the leading literati of whom Monsignor Gaddi considered himself a central figure. According to Benvenuto Cellini's *Autobiography*, Gaddi's literary circle consisted of "a certain Messer Giovanni, a Greek of eminent learning, Messer Ludovico of Fano, no less distinguished as a man of letters, Messer Antonio Allegretti, and Messer Annibal Caro, at that time in his early manhood."[1] (Cellini, Sebastiano del Piombo and Cardinal Bembo were all friends of Gaddi and the members of his household). Gaddi was widely known for his patronage in the publication of classical and contemporary authors. The famous printer Antonio Blado d'Asola (represented in the play under the pseudonym Barbagrigia) in 1531 dedicated his edition of Machiavelli's *Discourses* to Gaddi (calling him "master and benefactor"), and in 1532 his edition of Machiavelli's *Histories*. In the same year the printer Bernardo di Giunta dedicated to him the first

Florentine edition of *The Prince*. Undoubtedly Monsignor Gaddi achieved his many publications of classical authors by entrusting them to the members of his literary circle (including Caro), for he seems to have had little skill of his own in these matters. Cellini reports that "Messer Giovanni Gaddi . . . took great pleasure in favouring persons with talent, although he had no talent whatsoever himself."[2] Perhaps Gaddi's own limitations were part of the cause for Caro's dissatisfaction, expressed so frequently in his letters from this period, and the reason for his repeated attempts to leave the Monsignor's service. Before Gaddi's death in 1542, however, he succeeded only in gaining a three month's transfer (extended to a year) into the service of Monsignor Guidiccioni, Bishop of Fossombrone, President of Romagna, Governor of the Marca and close friend to the Farnese family.

Guidiccioni was a vital figure in Caro's career, for it was through his offices, at the time of Gaddi's death, that Caro became a member of the secretariat of Pierluigi Farnese, the eldest son of Pope Paul III. On behalf of Pierluigi, Caro undertook a series of diplomatic missions in Lombardy, France and Flanders, and when, in 1545, Pierluigi was granted the duchies of Parma and Piacenza, Caro was named administrator of justice in Piacenza.

The assassination of Pierluigi Farnese in 1547 brought that portion of Caro's career to an abrupt halt; accused of complicity in the plot and grand larceny, he was forced to leave Piacenza in haste. Once again in Rome, he entered the secretariat of the powerful Cardinal Alessandro Farnese, nephew of the Pope, in whose service he remained until 1563. The remainder of his days he spent in retirement with his family in a small villa in Frascati. He died November 20, 1566.

Literary Production

Annibal Caro was an accomplished poet, a skilful and elegant translator of Latin and Greek, an experienced collector of coins and archaeological rarities and a comic writer of enormous talent. His *Canzoniere*, commissioned in 1553 by Alessandro Farnese in praise of the house of France, is a work of some one hundred sonnets and five canzoni; among them is the famous "Venite all'ombra dei gran gigli d'oro" (Come Under the Shade of the Great Golden Lilies), which brought so much censure from the humanist Ludovico Castelvetro. Caro answered him in the *Apologia degli Accademici di Banchi* (Parma, 1558) in which he refuted Castelvetro's criticism and in turn accused him of heresy. The allegations were found to be false, but they were sufficiently embarrassing to force Castelvetro to leave Modena and then Italy. While a member of the semi-serious Roman Academy of Virtue, Caro composed a series of licentious parodies: *Comento di ser Agresto da Ficaruolo sopra la prima ficata del Padre Siceo; Nasea ovvero Diceria de' Nasi; Statua della Foia ovvero di Santa Nafissa*. His many letters, famous for their elegant style, were first printed in Venice in 1572-74. His translation of Virgil's *Aeneid* was until recently a standard text in Italian schools. His other translations include Longus' *Daphnis and Cloe* and Aristotle's *Rhetoric*.

History of the Text

Caro's only play was commissioned in 1543 by Pierluigi Farnese; it was revised and approved the following year by Benedetto Varchi (later employed by Benvenuto Cellini as redactor of his *Autobiography*). Yet the play never saw a performance, largely because of Caro's departure on a series of diplomatic missions and because of Pierluigi's removal to Parma in 1544. After the Duke's death in 1547, Caro refused a number of requests not only to stage the play, but even to have it copied for Pierluigi's daughter Vittoria, wife of Guidobaldo della Rovere of Urbino, on the grounds that *Gli Straccioni* was "composed for Rome and for that particular time and about a subject which at the time was still fresh and in accordance with the tastes of the Duke your father — may his memory be preserved forever — with whose participation it was in such a manner written."[3] Only eight years later did he relent and send a copy to the Court of

Urbino with the understanding that it would not be recopied or circulated elsewhere. Even after his retirement he refused permission to his old patron Alessandro Farnese to stage the play. It was first published in 1582 in an edition full of errors and lacunae due to censorship. It was not edited according to the original manuscript (Vaticano Urbinate 764) until 1942.

The Play

Near the end of the Prologue to the comedy, the author's spokesman informs his auditors, in a sort of apology, that the author "knows he's got a hard task on his hands, that he engaged in it out of obedience and not out of presumption." Undoubtedly *Gli Straccioni* would not have been written had it not been commissioned by Pierluigi. That it was completed on June 28, 1543, just a few months after Caro entered his service, suggests that the composition of the play may have been one of the conditions of his employment. As Caro's letters reveal, Pierluigi took a great personal interest in the writing of the play, perhaps to the extent of dictating the nature of at least some of its contents. Moreover, a special status is accorded to the play by the degree of secrecy which Pierluigi enjoins Caro to keep. This is made clear in a letter to Benedetto Varchi of March 13, 1544, in which Caro asks for his critical opinions on the work and for certain revisions to the language:

> I desire you to see my comedy only that I may improve it. Yet I must speak to you honestly: I know how compliant you are to your friends' wishes, which makes me worry that you will let this play out of your own hands. If this were to happen it would do me great harm, for my commission is strict and binding. Just the same, I am determined to send it to you and will have a copy of it made. I beg you, Messer Benedetto, make sure you do not wrong me. I know you will keep your word. But since you could be deceived by someone promising you the same, resolve to show it to no one, not even to mention its subject matter. As soon as it is copied I will send it to you.[4]

Caro's insistence upon the strictness of his commission, and the necessity of secrecy, go rather beyond what one would expect for a piece of light entertainment or carnival theatre. To be sure, it would spoil the fun if all the scenes and characters that the author had prepared for novelty's sake had been divulged to the audience before the actual presentation. Or again, if the play was intended as a commendatory piece for the Farnese family to be presented as a surprise on a given occasion, yet the need for secrecy would not be urged in such terms as Caro uses in his letter. Moreoever, these explanations do not account for Pierluigi's actual participation in the writing of the play. Surely Caro required no help, for his reputation was already substantial as a comic writer. Pierluigi's interference can only be explained by an intention on his part to make the play more than a mere *divertissement*. A case must be made for the hypothesis that Caro's task was to invest the patterns of erudite comedy with themes related to matters of state according to a grand cultural strategy which was at the centre of Farnese rule in Rome. As a play in the tradition of the *commedia erudita, Gli Straccioni* is a representative of the tradition at its height. But as a play in which serious political themes are so incorporated that they become significant determining factors in the design of the comic structure itself, Caro's comedy is perhaps unique.

The manifestations of that cultural strategy most easily recognized in the play are the several allusions to specific projects and institutions associated with a campaign by the Farnese family, headed by Pope Paul III, to establish a new order in the city of Rome and the Papal States, encompassing both physical improvements and judicial reform.[5] As we shall see, the play takes place quite self-consciously in a renovated Rome and the *dénouement* of the fable is brought about by a lawyer acting in the new spirit of Farnese justice. This program was part of a larger one to renew the image of Rome and the church abroad. Its waning prestige, due largely to the Lutheran invectives aimed against the corruption of Rome and the Curia, was the broader factor inciting Pope Paul to unite his ambitions for the universal church with his ambitions for the beautification of the city; the one was closely related to the other. In a sense, the construction of a new palace contributed to the greater glory and, indeed, credibility of Christendom. This new self-examining approach followed the failure of such *ex cathedra* tactics as the bull *Exsurge Domini* of 1520 in which Luther's teachings were handled with simple condemnation. In 1527, under Clement VII, Rome endured both spiritual humiliation and physical degradation at the hands of the Imperial Army which, with the complicity of the powerful Colonna family, ransacked the city. Perhaps no other single event did more to bring about the physical renewal of the city and a change in policy in the handling of affairs with countries to the north. At the time of Caro's appointment Pope Paul was trying to answer these challenges to the Church more decisively, by calling together a general council. The momentous Council of Trent was the grand climax of the Farnese reform movement.

In order to regain credibility, a new regime was deemed essential, one in which private acts of violence and the misuse of authority would be curbed, one which would especially halt the unbridled license of the nobility. The program included stricter laws, increased power for the courts, an order that all feudal landholders dwell within the city walls, provisions for a new census bureau, and the liberalization of trade.[6] Clearly implied in the program was a renewed bid to centralize more power in the hands of the Pope and his immediate family by diminishing the power of the nobility (hence the bestowal of Piacenza and Parma on Pierluigi and the Duchy of Castro on Ottaviano, Paul III's grandson). Pierluigi himself, accompanied by his friend Monsignor Guidiccioni, led the Papal troops victoriously against the insurgent Ascanio Colonna in the so-called Salt War of 1542 (provoked by the Pope's using his unique prerogatives as a spiritual leader as a means of centralizing his temporal powers).[7] The plan for reform, in short, touched upon virtually all spheres of life. At its centre was a powerful ruling family which sought, ideally, to combine enlightened rule with the creation of a society after its own image and according to its own dictates. In a sense, Rome was on its way to becoming a monument to the Farnese; such an impression of Roman life is abundantly expressed in the play. Even comic form, like everything else in Rome, was adapted and made to serve the Farnese cause. The special quality of the play, then, is the manner in which Caro's patron not only commissions a play, but dictates the degree to which it must be a calculated eulogy of the Farnese family and its reform measures.

Yet another tie with contemporary concerns is manifested by the implicit allusion in the title of the play to the uprising in 1531 of the *straccioni*, the poor of the city of Lucca. Monsignor Guidiccioni in 1531-32 wrote his famous *Orazione ai nobili di Lucca* defending the uprising.[8] Caro, who had been in his service, certainly knew of this document and its important place in Farnese policy. The title is therefore no coincidence, but a deliberate allusion to an episode of lasting importance and long-lived currency. The two scruffy scoundrels of Caro's comedy are not to be compared with the wretched poor who revolted against Sienese authority. Guidiccioni's *straccioni* are the truly impoverished of the times, people without means and without rights, unwilling slaves of the wealthy. On the other hand, the *straccioni* of the play are two half-crazed noblemen who assume the clothes of beggars in protest against their unsuccessful litigation — their failure to receive compensation for the jewels they had given to the Bank of San Giorgio. "For wretched malcontents like us, no finer attire will serve" (I.ii) one of them says, thus making themselves the objects of sarcasm and ridicule. Their melancholy state also derives from the stubbornness and irrationality of their refusal to allow the marriage of Giulietta, which led in turn to her abduction and disappearance. Thus the title, with its allusion to Guidiccioni's *Oration*, emphasizes the contrast between the world of the truly wretched and the extravagantly self-indulgent wretchedness of these two misers from Chios.

Again, the common denominator is the renovation of the judicial system under the Farnese reforms. The excessive behaviour of the two brothers, which had become the norm amongst the Roman aristocracy, was, despite Caro's light burlesqueing of it, the implicit target of serious attack.

The extravagance of Rome and its citizens is the keynote of the Prologue:

> For the moment you need only to know that these three circumstances will give rise to the most astonishing accidents of fortune involving men of diverse statures, wits and characters: dead ones who are alive, live ones who are dead, madmen who are wise, widowers who are married, husbands who have two wives and wives who have two husbands. You'll see visible phantoms, kith not known by their kin, relatives who are enemies, prisoners who are free, and such like *extravagances* and novelties. (our italics)

The exteme novelty of situation and the remarkable coincidences of erudite or learned comedy are compounded with a commentary on the extraordinarily corrupt social conditions of sixteenth-century Rome.

> DEMETRIO: But why are they parading in those motley trappings? Are they off their rockers? Not that that makes any difference in Rome.

The two scruffy brothers, creations of pure comedy, are also paradigms of the decadence of a Rome in need of discipline and reform. Caro turns comic conventions into social criticism, allowing for a successful amalgamation of his interests as a comic writer with those of Pierluigi the propagandist and reformer.

A second and related motif is the eulogistic theme featuring the Pauline restoration of the physical city of Rome as *caput mundi*. Paul III had promoted extensive renovations to the streets and buildings, given the order for slums to be cleared away, for new piazzas to be created, for standing water to be drained and for streets to be widened. Upon his return to Rome, Pilucca is totally disoriented: "Wait a minute. Where are we now? And what piazza is this? I never saw this street before, nor this one either." (I.i) His confusion serves to introduce a comic element — a Roman lost in his own home town. But it also calls attention to the many changes, to the destruction of the old Rome and the building of the new. The city itself is at the center of the play, the subject of radically contrasting impressions. The scruffy scoundrels comment in their way on the old Rome:

> GIOVANNI: Rome, sacred and holy? It's Rome of the fiend.
>
> BATTISTA: The very devil's Rome, gutless Rome.
>
> GIOVANNI: Rome impoverished and lunatic. (I.ii)

The impression is coloured by their disgruntled state just as was Pilucca's by his drunkenness, but underlying it are the topical "truths." Pilucca was a witness of the harmonious new Rome symbolized by the new Farnese Palace, a new Rome apostrophized in the words of Demetrio: "What a beautiful palace! What a splendid piazza! Oh, magnificent Rome." (I.i) The reference to Boccaccio, the "chief wallbanger . . . the lieutenant of earthquakes, the one who reduces residences to rubble with his bloody rod and magic thread" (I.i) is more than incidental. He is the contractor who has become the almost magic embodiment of the creative destructiveness of the Farnese. The Rome of justice, order, security and beauty, a tribute to Farnese vision, co-exists with a squalid, decadent, corrupt and bankrupt Rome. It is the comic order of the play itself that brings the Rome of law and order into the ascendant, allowing her to triumph over the criminal, neurotic and extravagant.

A close look at the play reveals how thoroughly the two themes are present: the comic-extravagant and the political-eulogistic.[9] Although Tindaro comes from a well-established and respected family, he has been refused permission to marry Giulietta. The two flee from Chios together; Giulietta, in consequence, falls into the hands of the Turks, is sold as a slave to Marabeo and is finally handed over to Jordano, Marabeo's wealthy master, for his private sexual pleasures. She is beyond conventional comic rescue either by her devoted but passive lover who assumes her to be dead, or by loyal servants. She is ultimately at the mercy of whatever justice the city of Rome can proffer her. Once in the streets, she dares to cry out in expectation of succour. It is the attorney, the representative of the Pope's justice, who comes to her rescue. This attorney stands apart from all the other characters of the play; he is level-headed and reasonable. He behaves professionally according to the principles and laws of the Farnese whom he serves.

Through the attorney's intervention the plot is brought to a satisfactory conclusion: he arranges for the reunion of Giulietta and Tindaro, for the repayment of the money owing to the *straccioni*, and for the punishment of the guilty. By the authority of the Farnese vested in him, happiness is restored and justice is dispensed to all. In short, the goals of comedy and of Farnese reform are realized simultaneously in a single *dénouement*; the conditions for achieving comic order are those created by the reform Pope, his ministers and officials. The theme comes close to the surface when the attorney declares, "To think of such assaults on a virgin, in Rome, in the Piazza Farnese, in the time of Pope Paul III and with the Pope here, now, in this very palace. But you're safe now, my child, don't worry. This villain will be punished." (IV, iv) The importance of such references confirms Caro's own later demur that the play was written for Rome, for a particular time and about a subject then fresh in the minds of his intended audience. Caro succeeds in adapting, without damaging the comic order itself, the structure of regular comedy to a tribute to the achievements and pretensions of the ruling dynasty which he served.

Plot

A fundamental question to be asked is whether this play follows in the tradition of the erudite comedy characterized by tightly planned, fast moving intrigue plots. From one vantage point, *The Scruffy Scoundrels* would appear to be no more than a series of unrelated scenes and sketches grouped around a highly conventionalized and loosely structured love plot: the arrival of Pilucca and Tindaro in Rome abounding in topical references; the appearance of the two ragged brothers so arbitrarily related to the rest of the events of the play; the love squabble between two servants that leads to Nuta's memorably comic invective; the stock farcical routines of the Mirandola episodes; the long pathetic tale of Tindaro so little of which actually takes place on the stage. There is a sense in which each scene contains its own ethos and milieu and hails from a particular comic genre, each with its own *topoi* and character types. The prank played on Mirandola is a farcical interlude that has no apparent causal bearing on the general plot. Nuta threatens to expose Marabeo by taking news of his illegal affairs to the Governor, but she never carries out her threat. The two brothers' litigation with the Grimaldi which, in one light, forms a kind of frame plot to the whole play is, in another, merely perfunctory. The tale of the long-lost niece, if extrapolated, is rather sketchy and, moreover, is so conventional a comic device that the reader is little inclined to give it much consideration. Yet Caro announces and defends an experimental and more complex approach to comic plotting in his Preface to this play that must be heard out before final judgement can be passed. Briefly, he makes a case for the triple plot, a procedure which contradicts both classical and contemporary rules requiring a single or, at most, a double plot. That fact alone goes far in explaining the apparent disunity and diversity of the plot elements.

In the Prologue Caro offers a rather outspoken defense of his practice, attacking his critics and praising his own originality:

> The constipated traditionalist may take offense at the
> triple plot, since the ancients never went beyond a single
> or a double one. But don't forget that though there are
> no existing precedents for our procedure, neither are
> there prohibitions against it. . . . Note that he [Caro]
> has followed the traditions in other areas. And in any
> case, change is inevitable since actions and the laws of
> actions depend on the times and fashions, and these
> change with every age. (Prologue)

His tone is suitably aggressive for the defense of a major
innovation under attack. But only the façade is dealt with,
the mere fact of the addition of a third plot, as if that alone
explained all. Caro does not hint at more fundamental
aesthetic or thematic motivations underlying his innovation.
Was he attempting to extend the range of a somewhat rule-
bound comic form, introduce a greater variety of characters,
fuse pre-existing comic forms in a single work, or design an
even more complex comic intrigue? Or was he merely multi-
plying the obvious in a mechanical way for the sake of the
novelty and in an effort simply to be controversial? The
more one familiarizes oneself with the text, the more one
sees possibilities for each of these propositions, each one
furnishing a critical entry into the play.

There is a rationale to be made for the choice of the
three plots. Caro was concerned that his situations be
plausible and identifiable to a contemporary audience, yet
he wished to respect the conventional rules of the learned
comedy and its traditions. Perhaps it is the care and skill that
he had to exercise in bringing these two demanding criteria
together into a single work that would make him write in
one of his letters that a successful comedy is "one of the most
tiring poems one could ever compose."[10] Erudite comedy
with its typologies had to be made contemporary, and the
contemporary had to be implanted in the play. The triple
plot was one procedure leading in this direction. Thus, one
of Caro's plots is drawn from an event in contemporary life,
a second is taken from a little-known Greek romance, while
the third is a familiar plot-pattern in the traditional theatre.

By such means he was able to satisfy the conventions of learned comedy, yet extend the play in terms of its representation of current affairs. Put another way, Caro was sent in the direction of extending the number and kinds of plot elements in his play by the very fact that he was attempting to satisfy two masters: his patron and the rules of regular comedy.

The two *straccioni* who give the comedy its title and the account of their litigation with the Grimaldi are derived from contemporary Roman life. The speaker of the Prologue plays on the fact: "Most of you out there in the audience must have known the scruffy scoundrels, the two brothers from Chios, Giovanni and Battista. . . . They always used to walk together in Rome. . . ." Once again the real and fictional are joined: Rome, familiar to all, was the express setting for this play with all its incredible events and far-fetched intrigues. A further example of the fusion of contemporary life with the theatrical is the introduction of Mirandola, crazy, and, in a larger sense, a figure symbolizing madness itself. Mirandola was, in fact, an historical figure; the audience would have recognized him as they would have recognized the scruffy brothers. Thus, the prank played on him by Ciullo, Fuligatto and Lispa (II.v.), though quite absurd, would have been acceptable to them in the context. On the other hand, Mirandola's confrontation with the two brothers (III.v.) is slapstick farce in the purest Boccaccian tradition and is justifiable only as a part of that literary genre.

The central plot derives almost entirely from the third century Greek romance by Achilles Tatius, *Leucippe and Cleitophon*: the escape of the two lovers from Chios, the shipwreck, Giulietta's abduction by pirates and her presumed death, the proposed marriage between Tindaro and a wealthy lady whose husband is also presumed dead, the reappearance of Giulietta and of the lady's husband and the final happy ending. The use of a Greek romance is in itself an innovation, but the actual material of such stories, including tales of abduction by pirates, had already become commonplace on the stage through the influence of Sienese comedies drawing on Boccaccio's tale of Gerbino from the Fourth Day of the *Decameron*.

The third plot, the discovery that Argentina is the long-lost daughter of Paolo, brother of the *straccioni*, completes the circle of recognitions and reunions; it is a motif derived from traditional comic theatre. A mark of Caro's artistry is his ability to work out a unified whole from such varied sources. With that achievement comes not only a more complex intrigue and novelty in the juxtaposing of literary allusions, but also a larger context for his thematic references.

The fragmentary appearance of the plotting is indeed mere appearance. Caro manages to link his comic vignettes through a complex pattern of family relationships and discoveries. The lawyer rehearses them all at the end, his very tediousness adding to the comic effect. He concludes with the two scruffy scoundrels who are, after all, "the fathers, uncles and fathers-in-law of Giulietta, Argentina, Jordano and Tindaro" (V.v.). Intrigue as complex as the audience could grasp and the maker could unravel with an acceptable minimum of plausibility was the nucleus of erudite comedy. Every writer strove for novelty in order to astonish his audience and so win approbation. Variety in unity was the intended goal. There is a degree of brinkmanship, but Caro understood the logistics of fine plotting; rapid changes of circumstances, impossible dilemmas, ironic confrontations, and an ingenious resolution. He was a master of the impasse, such as when Tindaro is accused by her uncles of murdering Giulietta at the very moment he is on the verge of marrying the "pregnant" widow. To flee Rome in order to escape the marriage is to admit guilt for the murder, to risk disgrace and imprisonment; to stay is to enter into marital strife and a cuckold's dishonour. We see further evidence of Caro's sense of architectonics in his balancing of the farcical with the sentimental: Nuta and Mirandola alternating scenes with Tindaro and Demetrio. These and many like devices, which the attentive reader will discover, serve to create a unified structure.

Finally, the plot contains in its design the universal themes of comedy. These come close to direct expression in the concluding words of the attorney: "Where there is union, let it be strengthened; where no union is possible, let love turn into charity. Now share the embrace all round." (V.v.) and in "Just see how much harmony has been born out of such confusion." (V.v.) These are sentences appropriate to the *dénouement* of romance comedy. Murder, rape, and polygamy are all narrowly avoided through the efforts of the attorney, liberally abetted by that goddess of comic plotting — good fortune. The plot is so conceived that all its tangled threads produce in the end both harmony and stasis: order is restored and nothing remains wanting resolution. A spirit of festival prevails where there is marriage, reunion, forgiveness and general rejoicing. The Farnese propaganda is handled not as a prescribed interpolation, but as a means for a simultaneous expression of these archetypal comic themes; given Caro's assignment the efficient management of plot is a measure of his comic genius.

Characters

Conventional plots entail conventional characters. The *commedia erudita* or regular comedy of the sixteenth century in Italy had settled on a number of character types, derived from classical Roman comedy, who reappeared in variant forms with predictable regularity: the crotchety parent, obstacle to the lovers' aspirations for marriage; the lovers themselves; the young lady's nurse or maid, usually a witty, down-to-earth realist who freely advised in matters of the heart; the young man's servant, often a clever pragmatist who worked out the schemes for tricking the old man or a rival lover; the bawd; the braggart soldier; the pedant; the doctor. Caro's play lacks such characters almost entirely. To be sure, there are the young lovers, but their cases are desperate until the end, the one lost in slavery, the other thinking the first one dead. There are no obstinate parents of the conventional sort, no witty servants whose efforts in aiding their masters make them the true *machinatori* or trickster-intriguers of the play, no bawds, no doctors or pedants, no braggart soldiers. The hero who is resurrected in the person of the corrupt and aggressive Jordano is an embodiment of the aristocratic vices that Pope Paul III wished to restrain. He is unrelated to the conventional hero of the theatre:

> Cavaliere, if you behave so lightly and irresponsibly during the reign of this Pope, whatever head you have left will be chopped off. Your boldness has been excessive; you have created a private prison in the city of Rome, treated women brutally, attempted murder. Your behaviour shows nothing but contempt for so lofty a prince. (V.v.)

Marabeo is Argentina's drunken and dishonest steward whose talents run towards violence and theft. Pilucca returns to take up his old position in order to embezzle funds from his master. They are not conventional servants, but additional figures representing the greed and corruption to which Rome had fallen. Marabeo sums up his philosophy: "That business of conscience and loyalty, it's fine for those who don't mind dying of hunger and cold. Riches, Pilucca, wealth, if it's a gentleman you want to be" (I.iv.). They get away with light penalties at the end only because a chastened Jordano realizes that they are merely by-products of the corruption of his own class and so pleads for their escape in order not to spoil the holiday climate.

Of Tindaro, Demetrio and Satiro little need be added. Their origins in the central plot of Tatius' *Leucippe and Cleitophon* accounts largely for the essence of their character types. Caro calls his main protagonist Tindaro/Gisippo, his friend Demetrio, and his servant Satiro. Caro's Tindaro suffers the same vicissitudes as Cleitophon, who also has a servant named Satyrus, who speaks the same pathetic language and who is faithfully in love and thus resists the sexual advances of a second woman (Argentina in *Gli Straccioni*, Melitte in Tatius' romance). But whereas Cleitophon resists because he does not believe Leucippe is dead, Tindaro resists because he wishes to remain faithful to Giulietta's memory, both in body and in spirit. This was a

new dimension with Caro and sets the style for many sentimental variants and parodies in later drama. Contemporary
comedy, however, did play a part in the formation of these
characters. In a play entitled *L'amicizia* (*The Friendship*),
staged between 1502 and 1512, Jacopo Nardi had introduced
the theme of friendship in retelling the story of Gisippo and
Tito found in the *Decameron* (X.I.). The same Nardi,
retelling the fifth tale of the fifth day of the *Decameron*,
wrote *I due felici rivali* (*The Two Happy Rivals*), staged in
Florence, February 1513, using the classical names of
Tindaro and Satiro. In Caro's play, Demetrio's harangues
that Tindaro marry the widow because of the debt of loyalty
and consideration Tindaro owes to him merely follow in a
long tradition of set speeches on the obligations of friendship. The link with Nardi is almost certain.

The minor characters derive from a mixture of sources
— historical and literary. The two brothers, as we mentioned
earlier, were well-known figures about Rome. Caro stylized
them and turned them into stage buffoons without clouding
their identities. Fuligatto, Ciullo and Lispa are represented
as typical Roman bullies. Of Mirandola, Caro speaks in
several of his letters as if he were a well-known lunatic.
There is the letter of 1535, with its allusions to the *Orlando
Furioso*, sent to Luigetto Castravillani in Africa:

> . . . and when you will climb the mountains of the moon
> remember to stay overnight with Enoch and Elias, from
> whom you will learn to carry out all the deeds you are
> planning. Make sure they give you a large phial full of
> brains; since you plan so many undertakings, you'll
> need them. I would also like to have a little phial of
> them in order to be capable of describing your deeds
> and, if you agree, to retrieve Mirandola's senses, for he
> could come in quite handy against those greedy glutton
> Turks.[12]

The Language

Caro states in one of his letters that the true interest of
comedy does not rest in the subject but in the language: "the

subject matter is ordinary, since subject matters of comedies cannot be otherwise, and the rarity of the episodes does not make them any better. What makes them better is the beauty of the sentences and of the style."[13] This we are to understand was the most applauded aspect of the play, the reason it was considered one of the finest theatrical texts of its day. The desirability of theatre in the vernacular and comedy in prose was still under debate; the challenge lingered for some time to prove the suppleness and range of the native tongue and the appropriateness of prose on the stage. The measure of Caro's achievement can be taken from the following quotation by Alessandro Piccolomini, the renowed Sienese scholar, humanist and playwright who, in his *Annotazioni sulla Poetica di Aristotele* (Venice, 1575), lists Annibal Caro, together with Bibbiena, Ariosto, the *Intronati* and the *Infiammati*, as being among the "learned and wise men" who wrote their comedies in prose.[14]

The language of Caro's play is literary Tuscan, the vernacular which had by this time become the acknowledged Italian of men of culture. Even the typically Roman characters, Pilucca, Marabeo, Fuligatto and Ciullo, speak the language of traditional Tuscan comedy.[15] Worth noting is the highly theatrical quality of the dialogue, generally bright, terse and fast moving. There is a staccato effect in the exchanges with the servants, full of irony and allusions, which is particularly lively:

PIL: Ah, do you know her already?
DEM: No, but I heard someone talking about her.
PIL: What where they saying?
DEM: That she's a knock out.
PIC: A real knock out.
DEM: And loaded.
PIL: Really loaded.
DEM: High quality goods.
PIL: Very high.
DEM: And a fairly casual companion.
PIL: They went so far as to say that?
DEM: And pregnant too, which is just a touch further.
   (III.ii)

The high degree of realism and naturalness in the speeches reflecting the rapid give and take of daily chatter is in contrast, of course, to the contrived sentimentality of the passages in which Tindaro vents his extremes of passion. The juxtaposing of two such contrasting styles, the one drawn from contemporary language, the other from a conventionally inflated literary mode, reflects the same fusion of contemporary and literary elements that we noted above with respect to plot and characterization.

Even a discussion of the language of the play brings us back to the Farnese theme in an indirect way. Almost all of the characters indulge in exaggerated styles of speaking. The two brothers are poor and in rags simply because of a litigation, and they speak in perpetual hyperbole; it is good comic theatre. At the same time, however, the language is disembodied; it floats after them. No one listens to them and they do not listen to each other. Tindaro wanders through the play rapt in excessive grief; he speaks to the wind. The others merely wait out of politeness, then disarm and deflate him in a line or two. All the characters in the episodes with Mirandola speak at sixes and sevens. The dynamics of plot are created out of the characters' incapacity to understand each other. The two servants are excessively wily and malign, in comparison with the conventional comic servant, their language revealing their hardened profiteering attitudes. The real and feigned misunderstanding of words, the sentimentality, the terms of trickery and duping, together make up the language of comedy, and the excesses in the language underscore the extravagance to be found in manners and behaviour. The decadence is manifested in the very words of the characters. In opposition to all this confusion, to be sure, is the attorney who speaks in collected and rational terms. Through his command of language he penetrates the chaos and calls the assembly to order. He is neither the self-interested crafty trickster who unravels the plot, nor a *deus ex machina* in a conventional sense. He is simply the voice of order, good sense and the Pope. Caro, therefore, does more than follow the standard decorum of differentiating speaking styles between high characters and low. He also divides the extravagant misguided language of comic excess from the rational discourse which leads to legal justice, and the special justice dispensed through the resolution of comedy.

A Note on the Translation

For our translation we have consulted the three modern Italian editions of Caro's *Gli Straccioni*: A. Greco (Roma, 1966); M. Guglielminetti (Torino, 1967); N. Borsellino in his *Commedie del Cinquecento* (Milano, 1967): It is this last edition, generally considered the most authoritative, that we used as the foundation for our translation.

The main problems we faced in translating Caro were: clarity, especially in the stage directions almost completely missing in the original; the rendering of puns and *double entrendres*; the linguistic consistency of the characters. To eliminate potential confusion we decided to add such indications as asides and related stage directions where we believed them to be indispensable. In translating puns and *double entendres* we tried to preserve the spirit and verve of the original by searching for meaningful equivalents, offering literal translations in the end notes. A very few expressions were rendered literally in the text in order to preserve the original colour; explanations for these also appear in the notes. Since some of the major characters change levels of speech throughout the play, we were faced with the problem of remaining faithful to the original while trying to give consistency to the language of those characters. Once again we decided to remain faithful to the original.

Throughout, we employed contemporary idiomatic English, though something of the rambling conversational qualities of the original are preserved in imitative syntax. Certain sentences in the original text are complex and pretentious; we tried to reflect these qualities without resorting to merely verbatim renderings. We have sought to avoid a dry, strictly literal translation. At the same time, we have avoided making any special concessions in order to render the play more theatrical than it is already. In fact, Caro's play in its design and language is highly theatrical, and it was written specifically for the stage. Our only desire was to bring out, in our translation, the theatricality of the original.

Select Bibliography

Only brief mention of Annibal Caro can be found in English, mainly in histories of the Italian theatre or of Italian literature. Small selections of the play appear in translation (Act I scene iv and Act II scene i) in Marvin T. Herrick's *Italian Comedy of the Renaissance* (University of Illinois Press, 1960), pp. 145-149. The most important critical studies in Italian are: V. Cian's introduction to Annibal Caro, *Scritti scelti* (Milano, 1912); A. Garosci, "Ritratto di A. Caro," in *Il Baretti*, IV, 4 (aprile 1927); B. Croce, *Poesia popolare e poesia d'arte* (Bari, 1933); N. Sapegno, *Compendio di storia della letteratura italiana* (Firenze, 1963); A. Greco, *Annibal Caro. Cultura e poesia* (Rome, 1950); M. Guglielminetti, "Marino lettore ed interprete del Caro," in *Lettere Italiane* (1963), 485-490, later included in *Tecnica e invenzione nell'opera di Giambattista Marino* (Messina-Firenze, 1964); E. Bonora, *Il Cinquecento* (Milano: Garzanti, 1966); R. Scrivano, *Cinquecento minore* (Bologna, 1966); C. Dionisotti, "A. Caro e il Rinascimento," in *Cultura e scuola*, V (1966), 36-49, later included in *L'istituzione del teatro comico nel Rinascimento* (Napoli, 1976); M. Guglielminetti, *Petrarca fra Abelardo ed Eloisa e altri saggi di letteratura italiana* (Bari, 1969); R. Ramat, "Appunti per gli Straccioni," in *Saggi sul Rinascimento* (Firenze 1969); G. Ferroni, "*Mutazione*" e "*Riscontro*" nel teatro di Machiavelli e altri saggi sulla commedia del Cinquecento (Rome, 1972).

Notes to the Introduction

1. Benvenuto Cellini, *Autobiography*, trans. John Addington Symonds (New York, 1975), p. 114.

2. *Ibid.* Symonds' translation reads: "a great connoisseur of the arts, although he had no practical acquaintance with any." We prefer to translate the original *virtuosi, virtù* as "talented" and "talent."

3. Quoted in Nino Borsellino, *Rozzi e Intronati, Esperienze e forme di teatro dal "Decameron" al "Candelaio"* (Roma, 1974), p. 190.

4. *Lettere familiari*, a cura di A. Greco, Vol. I (Firenze, 1959), pp. 297-8.

5. This thesis is developed in an admirable way by Giulio Ferroni, *"Mutazione" e "Riscontro" nel teatro di Machiavelli e altri saggi sulla commedia del Cinquecento* (Roma, 1972), pp. 195-230.

6. *Ibid.*, pp. 199-200.

7. Paul III had unilaterally decided to raise the price of salt which the Perugians had been convinced by Pope Eugenius IV to buy solely from the Apostolic Chamber. The Perugians decided to call back Rudolfo, the chief member of the Baglioni family, who was in the service of Cosimo I de' Medici, and together with Ascanio Colonna to rise in revolt against the salt tax. See Jean Delumeau "Rome: Political and Administrative Centralization in the Papal States in the Sixteenth Century," in *The Late Italian Renaissance*, ed. E. Cochrane (New York, 1970), 287-304. See also Pastor, *Storia dei Papi*, Vol. V., pp. 216 ff., and C. Capasso, *Paolo III* (Messina, 1924), Vol. II

8. Edited by Carlo Dionisotti (Roma, 1945); see also his "Annibal Caro e il Rinascimento" in *Cultura e Scuola*, V (1966), pp. 26-35.

9. Ferroni studies at length the motif of extravagance, although he does not emphasize it as a counterpoint to the eulogistic motif. The motif should also be studied within the tradition of the world upside-down (adynaton).

10. *Lettere familiari*, Vol. II, p. 78.

11. See for example the *Decameron*, VIII. 3.

12. *Lettere familiari*, Vol. I, p. 28.

13 *Lettere familiari*, Vol. II, pp. 142-3.

14. See *Borsellino*, pp. 190-91.

15. In one of his letters to Luca Martini Caro asks for a list of Tuscan proverbs and witticisms for his comedy. *Lettere familiari*, Vol. I, p. 278.

THE SCRUFFY SCOUNDRELS

(Gli Straccioni)

a prose comedy

Dramatis Personae

GIOVANNI, BATTISTA, the scruffy scoundrels

GIULIETTA, daughter of one of them, also known as Agata or Agatina

TINDARO, lover of Giulietta, also known as Gisippo

DEMETRIO, friend of Tindaro

SATIRO, servant of Demetrio

MADONNA ARGENTINA, niece of the scruffy scoundrels

IL CAVALIER JORDANO, her husband

BARBAGRIGIA, friend of Madonna Argentina

MARABEO, steward of Madonna Argentina

PILUCCA, servant of Madonna Argentina

NUTA, maid of Madonna Argentina

MESSER ROSSELLO, attorney at law

MIRANDOLA, lunatic

CIULLO, LISPA, FULIGATTO, rogues of Campo di Fiore

Prologue

Most of you out there in the audience must have known the scruffy scoundrels, the two brothers from Chios, Giovanni and Battista, or I might say Giovanni-Battista, since they were like two persons fused into one or a single one split into two — you know what I mean. They were the very Avino-Avolio[1] of our times, with their long coats embroidered all over with skeins of thread and covered with patches one on top of the other. They always used to walk together in Rome — filthy fellows they were, with their long hair and hooked noses. The one was the spitting image of the other, the way they used to do the same things and speak at the same time, or one in echo of the other. No matter that one of them is dead now, for not even death can sever the pair of them. The survivor is dead in the one who has passed on, and the dead one lives in the one who is still alive. I offer as proof that sometimes neither hide nor hair can be found anywhere of the one still alive, while today, right here on our stage, you'll see them both in the flesh.

You've probably heard the merry tales about that immortal pair, Castor and Pollux[2], who made some arrangement or other between them about their birth, life and death together? Well, let's say they never died, that they've turned into our two brothers here. Ours are just as handsome and they're always doing the same things together — though to be honest they're just a bit filthier.

Consider them poor and insane if you will, but our author has made them both rich and wise. The reason that prompted him is itself quite hilarious. If I tell you now, please don't give it away. These two brothers, knowing that the author has been for many years in the service of such lofty patrons as the Farnese family,[3] have assumed he must be a pretty eminent figure himself. So, to solicit his favour, they have generously granted him 50,000 gold scudi,[4] money we all know they are still trying to get back from the Grimaldi.[5] Even so, the author, who has only imagined himself rich in his dreams, took these promises for real, and banked on them as if he had the cash in his hand. Like the chap who paid hard money for a feast of hot air,[6] he will have the scruffy brothers recover their 300,000 scudi in this comedy of his, in exchange for the 50,000 scudi he received from them in words. He's done the same thing for their intellects; insofar as they have taken him for a great man he has billed them as wise men.

These two ghostly characters[7] who've given the play a name, have given it a subject too in three ways:[8] through a litigation they have with the Grimaldi, through a daughter they left in Chios, and through a niece they didn't known they had in Rome. In the course of the comedy you'll see the origin, unfolding and resolution of a whole maze of fears, deceits, jealousies and brawls. For the moment you need only know that these three circumstances will give rise to the most astonishing accidents of fortune involving men of diverse statures, wits and characters: dead ones who are alive, live ones who are dead, madmen who are wise, widowers who are married, husbands who have two wives and wives who have two husbands. You'll see visible phantoms, kith not known by their kin, relatives who are enemies, prisoners who are free, and such like extravagances and novelties. The constipated traditionalist may take offense at the triple plot, since the ancients never went beyond a single or double one. But don't forget that though there are no existing precedents for our procedure, neither are there prohibitions against it. And besides, the author didn't choose to do it without good reason. The tale requires three types of humours: if the audience is not moved by the first or relieved by the second, the third is sure to purge them because its subject matter is pleasant and consistent with the others.[9] All three are interwoven to form a single complete subject, though each one has its own parts and could alone constitute a comedy. To be

4

faultless and full of art is indeed praiseworthy, but our author is happy merely to escape reproof. Note that he has followed the traditions in other areas. And in any case, change is inevitable since actions and the laws of actions depend on the times and fashions, and these change with every age. If someone donned a purple-bordered toga today, no matter how fine he looked, he might as well have put on a flat cap and loose socks, since the current modes which dictate what appeals to men's eyes, ears and tastes, have declared against them both. There are just a few other things the author bids me say in his defense, namely, in short, that he knows he has a hard task on his hands, that he engaged in it out of obedience and not out of presumption, and that he has tried his level best to please. There's no such thing as an established set of rules for comedy, anyway; the models are legion, everyone has his own head, every head has its own ideas, and every idea has its reasons. So to please everyone is difficult, he realizes, and to do so in all respects is downright impossible. Therefore, simply to please you in part is sufficient recompense for his labours. Lend us a favourable ear. Sit back and enjoy yourselves. Since many a dish will be served up in the banquet to follow, I trust there will be meat for one and all.

ACT I

SCENE I

DEMETRIO: Since I've been your faithful companion through such bad times on the high seas, Pilucca, don't abandon me on land, now that the times are good. I'm a stranger here in Rome, and I need someone to show me around until I find this Messer Tindaro I was telling you about. Are you with me?

PILUCCA: What? Before we even lift a glass or two?

DEMETRIO: Come on. You had quite a few when we were in Ripa.[10]

PILUCCA: Uh huh — and since then?

DEMETRIO: Well at least tell me where I might run into him.

PILUCCA: Everybody turns up at Ponte,[11] one time or another.

DEMETRIO: And where is Ponte, then?

PILUCCA: Wait a minute. Where are we now? And what piazza is this? I've never seen this street before, nor this one either.

DEMETRIO: Don't tell me we need a compass on land too.

PILUCCA: Where's the Farnese palace,[12] anyway?

DEMETRIO: If it were a grog shop we'd have found it by now.

PILUCCA: Maybe this is it? No, it wasn't so high.

DEMETRIO: At being high, you're the winner.

PILUCCA: Still, it could be it. In fact, it is. But where is my mistress's house? It used to be right across the way.

DEMETRIO: (*aside*) He's got as many loops in his brain as he has barrels in his belly.

PILUCCA: I could have sworn it was here.

PILUCCA: Greco?[13]

PILUCCA: No, farther along.

DEMETRIO: Corso?[14]

PILUCCA: On the other side.

DEMETRIO: Mazzacane?[15]

PILUCCA: Wait, where is Campo di Fiori?[16] This way or that way?

DEMETRIO: Well at least you might recognize some of the people around here.

PILUCCA: Hey, hey, it's the printer's shop . . . what's his name . . . Barbagrigia.[17]

BARBAGRIGIA: Welcome, welcome.

PILUCCA: Well, well! How are things with you?

BARBAGRIGIA: Bulging at the seams, as you can see.

PILUCCA: I can see it quite well. That drum of a belly you've put on barely lets you through the door, God bless it.

BARBAGRIGIA: (*aside*) He's all insults and presumptiousness. — Who are you, anyway?

PILUCCA: Me? I'm Pilucca.

BARBAGRIGIA: What? Pilucca? How come you look so scrawny?[18]

DEMETRIO: (*aside*) There's tit for tat.

BARBAGRIGIA: So what's this get-up all about? You look like a jailbird.

PILUCCA: It came by destiny, not felony.

BARBAGRIGIA: It's not the last time you'll be there.

DEMETRIO: He means the police will be after you in no time.

PILUCCA: His meaning is perfectly clear.

BARBAGRIGIA: So what happened to you, anyway?

PILUCCA: You remember that your good friend the Cavaliere decided to go to the Near East in order to collect some sort of inheritance for my mistress?

BARBAGRIGIA: Like it was yesterday.

PILUCCA: And that we haven't heard a word from him since he left?

BARBAGRIGIA: That too.

PILUCCA: And that my mistress sent me to the corners of the globe looking for him?

BARBAGRIGIA: Wise decision.

PILUCCA: Well, I didn't find him and damned near lost myself in the process.

BARBAGRIGIA: You fell into the hands of the Moors eh?[19] Well, the gain was entirely ours.

PILUCCA: Five cursed years.

BARBAGRIGIA: I know the rest — an oar thirty feet long.

PILUCCA: Worse.

BARBAGRIGIA: Fifty pound chains?

PILUCCA: Worse than that.

BARBAGRIGIA: As many lashes as there are grains of sand?

PILLUCA: Even worse.

BARBAGRIGIA: Swarms of lice?

PILUCCA: Worse, I'm telling you.

BARBAGRIGIA: What the devil can be worse?

PILUCCA: Hardtack and water.

BARBAGRIGIA: Uh huh, and how did you manage to escape?

PILUCCA: The devil be thanked, down she went, straight to the bottom at last; only this gentleman and I managed to get out in time.

BARBAGRIGIA: Ergo, their misfortune was really your good fortune.

PILUCCA: Enough of all that, we're here now — though where that is I don't exactly know. I'm out of the sea, but my head's still adrift. I have to confess I can't even find the house of Madonna Argentina, my mistress.

BARBAGRIGIA: Ha, ha!

PILUCCA: Where the devil has it gone to?

BARBAGRIGIA: Boccaccio swallowed it.

PILUCCA: Boccaccio who?

BARBAGRIGIA: The chief wall-banger, you know who I mean, the lieutenant of earthquakes, the one who reduces residences to rubble with his bloody rod and magic thread.[20]

PILUCCA: Oh, right, right, the one with the glasses; he's a good friend of my mistress.

BARBAGRIGIA: Just the reason he did her the favour of shoving her house into the piazza.

PILUCCA: Her house into the piazza? Not into this one.

BARBAGRIGIA: Ha, ha!

PILUCCA: I get it; what an idiot I am. Well, there could be no greater glory than falling to make way for a work of such splendour.[21]

DEMETRIO: What a beautiful palace! What a splendid piazza! Oh, magnificent Rome!

PILUCCA: Well, what shall I do? The house is gone, my mistress is lost, I'm starved half-blind and I'm terrified of water. I won't feel safe until I've gained my mistress' cellar.

BARBAGRIGIA: There the risk of drowning is even greater.

PILUCCA: You're cutting my throat by degrees; just show me the way.

BARBAGRIGIA: So where did you go, after all, in search of the Cavaliere?

PILUCCA: To the brink of the other world.

BARBAGRIGIA: And after all that you never found him?

PILUCCA: How could I if he's dead?

BARBAGRIGIA: Oh my beloved friend, my poor friend. Where? How did he die?

PILUCCA: It's worth an epic and I'm starving.

BARBAGRIGIA: Tell me in a word or two.

PILUCCA: He just died, just like that. I think I mentioned my present famished state? Could you kindly direct me to the abode of my mistress?

BARBAGRIGIA: All right, let's go; you've been chastized enough. I'll accompany you. I want to hear the whole story and offer my condolences to our lady.

DEMETRIO: Don't we want to find that friend of mine first, Pilucca?

PILUCCA: How can I find somebody else when I'm lost myself?

BARBAGRIGIA: Who is it you're looking for my good man?

DEMETRIO: A Messer Tindaro from Chios; the trouble is that I'm not sure he's in Rome, though I can't think he's anywhere else.

PILUCCA: That will be worse than looking for mushrooms.

BARBAGRIGIA: I don't know of him, myself, but these two ragged scoundrels coming along are from Chios.

DEMETRIO: Just have a look at this honourable pair! You go on ahead, I want to ask them something.

PILUCCA: Right. I'll meet you later.

SCENE II   BATTISTA, GIOVANNI (scruffy scoundrels)
                      DEMETRIO

GIOVANNI: Rome, sacred and holy? It's the Rome of the
            fiend.

BATTISTA: The very devil's Rome, gutless Rome.

GIOVANNI: Rome, impoverished and lunatic.

BATTISTA: And the cause of all our poverty and madness.

GIOVANNI: With the benediction of God Almighty.

DEMETRIO: (*aside*) What kind of sneaking crows are these?
            They must be either brawlers or alchemists.

GIOVANNI: From Chios to Genoa.

BATTISTA: From Genoa to Rome.

GIOVANNI: From Herod to Pilate, from pillar to post.

BATTISTA: In the space of a day.

DEMETRIO: (*aside*) They're from Chios, all right, on their
            way from Genoa, and they're in a bit of a tiff. Let's wait
            and see if they're the Canali.

GIOVANNI: If it's true that Tindaro has abducted my
            daughter, Giulietta, we're even more shamed and humi-
            liated in the eyes of this town than we thought.

DEMETRIO: (*aside*) They're talking about Giulietta and
            Tindaro; they must be the ones. But why are they
            parading in these motley trappings? Are they crazy? Not
            that that makes any difference in Rome. Why are they
            acting so strangely? I wonder what's going on between
            these two. What do they know about Tindaro? I'd risk
            introducing myself, but they might suspect me of being
            Tindaro's accomplice in the kidnapping of Giulietta.
            Then again, they've never seen me. They don't know I'm
            Demetrio.

GIOVANNI: Look at that fellow's clothes; isn't he from the
            same country we are?[22]

BATTISTA: Where do you hail from, my friend?

DEMETRIO: From the east.

GIOVANNI: Which part?

DEMETRIO: From Chios.

BATTISTA: A true son of Chios?

DEMETRIO: At your command, and you?

GIOVANNI: Why, from Chios too.

DEMETRIO: What brings you here?

BATTISTA: Business, and you?

DEMETRIO: Mere chance. But may I ask, aren't you from the Canali family?

GIOVANNI: Indeed, we are.

DEMETRIO: But why the rags?

BATTISTA: The inheritance of poverty and our law suit.

DEMETRIO: By God, that's quite an honour you're paying yourselves.

GIOVANNI: For wretched malcontents like us, no finer attire will serve.

BATTISTA: Not until we've avenged ourselves against our abusers.

DEMETRIO: Who are they?

GIOVANNI: If you're from Chios you should know.

DEMETRIO: Oh yes, of course . . . uh Tindaro.

BATTISTA: Tindaro and Demetrio.

DEMETRIO: Why Demetrio? Isn't he one of your kin? Whatever he did must have been for your good and your daughter's too. And as for Tindaro, no one will deny he acted out of a teeming love for Giulietta.

GIOVANNI: A keen sense of our good, by God.

BATTISTA: And a teeming love it was.

13

GIOVANNI: To dishonour her.

BATTISTA: And to heap shame upon her entire family.

DEMETRIO: When a man seeks a wife and his love is honest, there's neither dishonour nor shame; he was moved not by contempt towards you but by the desire to be related to you.

GIOVANNI: In spite of us.

DEMETRIO: Out of good-will towards you.

BATTISTA: Like the nuns of Genoa he goes on his lark and then he asks permission.[23]

DEMETRIO: Well, you made it quite clear you were determined to say no.

GIOVANNI: Just because a person keeps saying no, it doesn't mean he can't say yes in the end, and that's just what we did.

DEMETRIO: Don't forget that for lovers, patience without hope turns into despair.

BATTISTA: And don't you forget that for the abused it turns into vendetta.

DEMETRIO: Do yourself a favor: accept what they've done and what God has ordained. This will remedy past grievances and those yet to come. And besides, why shouldn't you rejoice that your daughter has married the richest, the most noble and honest youth in Chios?

GIOVANNI: The rewards due his merits have been forfeited by his insolence.

BATTISTA: If he had proceeded properly without abducting her, she would have been his.

DEMETRIO: His she is now. And since there's no taking her back, what can you do but give her up to him?

GIOVANNI: Since he can't have her with honour, he won't have her with consent.

DEMETRIO: Quite the contrary. Since you can't stop the deed, how else can your honour be saved?

BATTISTA: Deed, indeed! It's a misdeed. Everyone will agree.

DEMETRIO: You're on the wrong path.

GIOVANNI: You're talking like one of their friends.

DEMETRIO: And one of yours, though you don't know me.

BATTISTA: What? Who are you?

DEMETRIO: Just wait. I'm sure we'll have the occasion to discuss the matter again, to the benefit of all.

GIOVANNI: More words on the matter we don't need. What we want to know is what's become of them.

DEMETRIO: I'm looking for them myself.

BATTISTA: In Rome?

DEMETRIO: No hints from me; your stubborness silences me.

GIOVANNI: We beseech you to tell us. For news of our beloved daughter we'll listen to anything you say.

DEMETRIO: Ah, that looks like Satiro strolling along. Adieu.

GIOVANNI: Where are you off to?

DEMETRIO: There's no more time for chatting.

BATTISTA: Listen, what's your name?

GIOVANNI: Where can we find you?

DEMETRIO: I can't stay a moment longer.

GIOVANNI: Say something more to help us.

DEMETRIO: All in good time. I'm off now. But where can I find you?

GIOVANNI: We're on our way to demand our due and then we'll come right back here.

DEMETRIO: Good. We'll talk later then.

SCENE III   DEMETRIO, GISIPPO (also known as
                        Tindaro), SATIRO

DEMETRIO: (*aside*) Satiro it is, by God. If only Messer
            Tindaro were here, this matter could be a sorted out.
            Wait a minute. It is Tindaro. What good fortune that I
            should meet them both today.

GISIPPO: A wife, my wife? Let's please not discuss it further.

DEMETRIO: (*aside*) His wife's Giulietta; could he be
            speaking of her? I'd better do some eavesdropping.

SATIRO: Your treatment of her is grossly unfair considering
            her great love for you.

GISIPPO: What greater wrong than to accept her love when
            my heart is filled with love for another.

DEMETRIO: (*aside*) Another? Odd that he should be rejecting
            Giulietta now after we kidnapped her, after we suffered
            condemnation, confinement and ruin to have her.

SATIRO: You'll live to regret it, master.

GISIPPO: Bah! You're boring me. You're prodding for an
            answer I can't give. You know I'm fond of you, but your
            harangues are getting pedantic and tiresome.

DEMETRIO: (*aside*) What's all this? I'd better find out what's
            going on.

GISIPPO: Satiro, can this really be Demetrio I'm seeing?

DEMETRIO: You can trust your eyes. It really is.

GISIPPO: Demetrio! My faithful friend!

SATIRO: Oh, Master!

DEMETRIO: Ah, good old Satiro, and Messer Tindaro, I've
            found you at last.

SATIRO: But I must tell you, Messer Tindaro here isn't
            Tindaro anymore.

GISIPPO: That's quite true. I've changed my name.

16

DEMETRIO: What's happened?

SATIRO: He now calls himself Gisippo.

DEMETRIO: Excellent! What a good idea.

GISIPPO: But where are you coming from and what are you
    doing here?

DEMETRIO: You might say I'm a true man of the world, I've
    been so many places. I've been looking for you and I've
    got some good news.

GISIPPO: Your presence alone is the best news you can
    bring.

DEMETRIO: I treasure your devotion, but I will treasure even
    more the fulfillment of all your hopes and dreams.

GISIPPO: Alas, they'll never come true.

DEMETRIO: How can that be now that you have your
    Giulietta?

GISIPPO: She's now no longer mine, nor will she ever be.

DEMETRIO: Holy saints, you're rejecting her now that her
    kinsmen have consented? Don't you know? As soon as
    we took her away, a letter arrived from her father and
    uncle here in Italy giving you permission to take her as
    your wife. Had we held off for a single day, the abduc-
    tion wouldn't have been necessary.

GISIPPO: Ah, fortune, fortune, these are your blows. The
    bad you send never misses the mark; the good ever goes
    astray, or arrives only when it is too late.

DEMETRIO: Her wretched mother, having received letters
    from here, was deeply grieved by your departure. When
    I heard that she was having you pursued, I sought you
    myself in order to share your destiny. Since my compli-
    city in the deed was discovered I have been persecuted
    by the courts, and even more by fortune. I have only just
    escaped the Moors and at long last, after much mishap,
    arrived in Rome. Here I encountered Giulietta's father
    and uncle and tried to reason with them. Judging by

what I found out, and by what I know from our own country, I can assure you that Giulietta will be yours with a universal blessing. Why are you crying, Messer Gisippo?

GISIPPO: Alas.

DEMETRIO: Satiro, what's the meaning of this?

GISIPPO: Alas, alas.

SATIRO: Don't you know that Giulietta is dead?

DEMETRIO: Dead? Giulietta? What are you saying, Satiro?

GISIPPO: While I enjoyed her love her family was my enemy; now that I have their blessing she is no longer mine. While alive she was denied me; now that she is dead, they bestow her upon me.

DEMETRIO: What an incalculable loss. You have reason enough to grieve. And yet, it is not meet that a man of your constancy and prudence should fall prey to despair for something which is natural, necessary and without remedy.

GISIPPO: Ah Demetrio. If only her death had been natural and necessary. Therein lies my grief. She was slain while still an innocent maid by the hand of heathen dogs; the cruellest of deaths she suffered, in my very presence, and the worst is that I myself was the cause of it. Ah, wretched Giulietta.

DEMETRIO: I feel my heart breaking. Oh, woe. What cruel destiny.

SATIRO: Best leave off, sir, or he will die of anguish. Let's give him a moment to recover himself.

DEMETRIO: Satiro, how did such a fell mishap come about?

SATIRO: In a word, after abducting Giulietta, we sailed for Corfu. Just as we gained sight of Zacintus we were attacked and captured by five Turkish vessels.[24] Messer Gisippo, hoping to find acquaintances in the island who

SCENE I
DEMETRIO, PILUCCA, BARBAGRIGIA

would ransom us, was put ashore along with myself in the early morning, leaving Giulietta behind. When we landed, we discovered that the galleons of the Venetians had newly arrived from Cefalonia.[25] He recognized the captain as a dear friend, and they determined between themselves to pursue and overcome the Turks, who had meanwhile set sail in flight. As we drew near, they tied Giulietta to the stern threatening murder in order to stop us, but their threats only redoubled our efforts. Then suddenly, before our very eyes, they chopped off her head and threw her body into the sea.

DEMETRIO: Those treacherous dogs.

SATIRO: Our galleons were delayed as Gisippo tried to recover the body, giving occasion to the Turks to slip away.

DEMETRIO: Ah, ill-fated maiden. Then who is the lady you spoke of before, the one he is now refusing to have?

SATIRO: Ah Master Demetrio, God has sent us this opportunity in recompense for so great a misfortune. A widow, a very wealthy noblewoman, the most gentle creature in Rome — it is natural that blood should seek kindred blood — no sooner had she seen him than she fell in love with him. She wants him as a husband and as lord over all her wealth. And what a fortune she has! And what a woman he would have! An estate like a fief, and a very goddess. You are aware of our condition. If he doesn't accept her, we'll go on wandering forever, but I can't hammer that into his head. Since you're here, why don't you give it a try?

DEMETRIO: Here? Now? Surely it's not the time to broach a subject like that. First let's try to assuage his anguish, and when he's better disposed, we'll speak to him about it.

SATIRO: But for now, let's be off. I see someone leaving the widow's house and I'm sure he's being sent to urge me to seal the marriage. I want to hold him off till we get matters more settled on our side.

19

DEMETRIO: I propose a stroll, Messer Gisippo. Since I'm in
Rome I'd like to see the city.

SCENE IV   PILUCCA, MARABEO, NUTA

PILUCCA: (*alone*) All the trifling questions my lady has put
to me have tired me right out. Four times already she's
had me summoned from the cellar, forcing me to repeat
at least a thousand times that the master is dead. You'd
think she was afraid of his resurrection. Right now I'm
worried about my own mortality. While she argues with
Barbagrigia, I've got my chance to tipple with the
steward and renew our pact to pilfer the mistress. There
he is now, standing at a window caressing his wine flask.
— Greetings, Marabeo, you charm the fog at midday.
Oh, Marabeo! (*to audience*) He's lost himself over the
brink of his glass, the lout. — Marabeo!

MARABEO: A wine with body and sparkling at the same
time. It's gone right down to the tips of my toes.

PILUCCA: Just think, if it ever got to his head! Marabeo!
May you drop dead.

MARABEO: Who's there?

PILUCCA: You don't recognize me, you old scoundrel?

MARABEO: Not I. Let me have another nip and then I'll be
down.

PILUCCA: May the devil take you since the flask will be
empty. (*to audience*) What's all the rumbling? Did he fall
down the stairs?

MARABEO: Oh, ow, I'm in agony.

PILUCCA: (*to audience*) His mouth still works. No harm
done if his neck's not broken.

MARABEO: My poor head!

PILUCCA: What have you got there? Take your hand away. Nothing. When it comes to your head, a bruise is the least of your problems. Go on, finish it off yourself.

MARABEO: Who the hell are you, coming along today and making me break my neck?

PILUCCA: You still don't know me? It's Pilucca.

MARABEO: From Lucca?

PILUCCA: No, I'm Pilucca.

MARABEO: Pilucca. Who'd've recognized you looking so frazzled out? Say! Did the master ever come back?

PILUCCA: Yes, he did.

MARABEO: The master has come back!

PILUCCA: The master has come back, yes.

MARABEO: So my neck really will be broken.

PILUCCA: Listen, I've been ordered to review your accounts. We have an agreement, you and I, if you know what I mean.

MARABEO: What do you think you'll count? Since you left, we haven't earned a penny.

PILUCCA: Marabeo, you know that I know you, and you know me. Besides being crooked by nature, I learned all my tricks from you, and I've just lately graduated from jail, so make up your mind. I'm not the type to be pushed around. Since we're in it so far together, we'd better both keep our mouths shut and go on aiding and abetting each other. I want my cut of everything you've pinched down to the last cent[26] or I'll mangle this vintage for you.

MARABEO: This whole business scares me senseless. I need somebody like you. I'll do whatever you say.

PILUCCA: Then I want in on all past and future proceeds.

MARABEO: Fair enough. The old arrangements as usual?

PILUCCA: With coin in the palm of my hand.

MARABEO: To settle the accounts?

PILUCCA: Yes, with real money.

MARABEO: Enough said. I'll see that you get it.

PILUCCA: I mean cash; give it to me now.

MARABEO: I give you my word.

PILUCCA: I can't spend that.

MARABEO: You'll get it. Believe me!

PILUCCA: All right, I'll trust you. But let me deserve the money, since I feel a twinge of conscience in pilfering it, by giving you the news of the master you were asking about.

MARABEO: Tell me he hasn't come back.

PILUCCA: He hasn't come back.

MARABEO: And that he'll never come back.

PILUCCA: He'll never come back.

MARABEO: And that he's dead.

PILUCCA: He's dead.

MARABEO: For real?

PILUCCA: Can someone be dead just for laughs?

MARABEO: Master Jordano is dead?

PILUCCA: Master Jordano.

MARABEO: At sea?

PILUCCA: At sea.

MARABEO: The sea beheld him and rolled back her waves. Jordan passed through, just like the Scriptures said.[27]

PILUCCA: If so, he deserved it.

MARABEO: And you deserve your money for such good news, Pilucca. And now I'll give you even better news.

22

PILUCCA: What can top the news of master's death?

MARABEO: I'll tell you: the mistress is in love.

PILUCCA: That's a good one! O ho, I get you; my news
secures all our past gains, yours sets up for the future.

MARABEO: You've got it. The mistress will have her love
and we two will look after her wealth. That business of
conscience and loyalty, it's fine for those who don't
mind dying of hunger and cold. Riches, Pilucca, wealth,
if it's a gentleman you want to be. Since our parents left
us nothing, and these others haven't sense enough to
give it to us, since we don't know the art of earning it,
and hard work is bad for our health, is it any surprise
that we make use of our hands? Anyway, the rope's a
better way to go than starvation. Are you with me,
Pilucca?

PILUCCA: Sounds like a good philosophy to me. Which
school is it — Pleuripathetics or Stoiters?[28]

MARABEO: I've got no use for all those alphabastards.[29] We
need more than chop-logic to live on. There comes Nuta
and she looks mad as hops.

NUTA: You damned lazy traitor. So that's why you didn't
want me in the house anymore. Once it was kidney
stones, then a lumbago, then cancer — may you get
them all for real.

MARABEO: What are you on about, Nuta?

NUTA: What am I on about? You swineskinned bastard.

MARABEO: Aie, my beard, aie!

PILUCCA: Ha, ha, ha!

NUTA: So it's fresh goods you wanted you decrepit old pig.
It'll make you putrid, I can tell you. Take a woman by
force, would you?

MARABEO: What woman?

NUTA: Everyone knows it, you filthy old tramp.

23

PILUCCA: Ha, ha, ha!

MARABEO: My Nuta.

NUTA: By force, eh?

MARABEO: Shut your trap, Nuta.

NUTA: I'll tell the whole world.

MARABEO: At least stop shouting so loud.

NUTA: Taking them by force, by force.

PILUCCA: Nice favour she's doing you, by God!

NUTA: By for. . .

MARABEO: Shut up.

NUTA: Try and stop me you old reprobate. I say it to spite
     you — a maid by force.

PILUCCA: If you want her quiet, tell her to yell.

MARABEO: My Nuta, sugarplum.

NUTA: Yours? You stinking dog.

MARABEO: Skin me alive, but please stop shouting.

NUTA: Nothing but a dirty old man.[30]

PILUCCA: Ha, ha, ha!

NUTA: If I didn't have to go back home now, I'd denounce
     you before the Governor.

MARABEO: Listen to me, Nuta. Make her stop, Pilucca.

PILUCCA: Nuta wait! Listen to just another word, Nuta.
     Just as I thought, the devil's taken her.

SCENE V   MARABEO, PILUCCA

MARABEO: Pilucca, I'm ruined.

PILUCCA: You've taken quite a thrashing.

MARABEO: It's worse than that.

PILUCCA: What kind of brawl is this?

MARABEO: Brawl, hell! It's a brawl leading straight to a hanging rope or a dungeon.

PILUCCA: Ah, send her to the devil.

MARABEO: You can laugh, but I'm scared out of my wits. You won't believe what a fix I'm in or the stupid blunder I've made.

PILUCCA: What's this great blunder of yours?

MARABEO: Keeping a woman against her will.

PILUCCA: Oh boy, you will flirt with the gallows. So who is this woman?

MARABEO: A young girl freed from the Turks by the Pope's galleys.

PILUCCA: And how did you come by her?

MARABEO: Here's the story: last summer our master's galleys sailed for the East as privateers against the infidels. On their return they engaged a Turkish fleet that had just escaped the Venetians, gained the victory, put the infidels in chains and, upon arrival at Civitavecchia, released their Christian prisoners, because according to perennial custom and the decree of his Holiness there can be no Christian slaves in Rome. Among those freed was this girl who calls herself Agata. But the captain who first captured her secretly held her back when the others were released. I happened to be in Civitavecchia at the time, and since the captain was a friend of mine, he showed me this slave of his. I liked her as much as I dislike all other women. The captain, short of money and as afraid to keep her as I am now, sold her to me on the promise that I wouldn't take her to Rome. But I broke my promise and brought her here anyway, hoping to keep her a secret. I thought I could win her over so that my lust would be provided for. But in spite of my caresses, threats, and the torments I've inflicted upon her, I haven't managed to gain one favourable look from her, and now, despite my vigilance, the secret has gotten out.

PILUCCA: Is she good looking?

MARABEO: She's beautiful, and good, and wonderfully intelligent. More than that, she's a Christian, free and apparently noble. Here I am, torn between the fear of keeping her, the despair of ever conquering her, and the grief of letting her go. How the secret leaked out I don't know. I'm totally confused; I've no idea how to escape prosecution. Not even the egg of the Ascension[31] could save me or the captain from prison, or worse, hanging, if the Governor ever found out. Are you really a true friend, Pilucca?

PILUCCA: What do you want me to do?

MARABEO: Get on the good side of this tattle-tale Nuta. Find out if she's blabbed the news abroad, or make sure she doesn't if it isn't too late and, above all, see that she doesn't go to the Governor. Then we'll think of some way out of this scrape.

PILUCCA: Come on, you can put your mind at rest. I'll go and have a little chat with Nuta about all this.

MARABEO: And I'll talk to Agatina, just in case she knows something.

ACT II

SCENE I BARBAGRIGIA, GISIPPO, DEMETRIO, SATIRO, NUTA

BARBAGRIGIA: (*alone*) Oh blessed be this dear friend of mine! At least she says what she thinks, and she thinks straight as far as I can see. Now that Pilucca has assured her that her husband is dead, she says she wants another one — young, a foreigner, one without means of his own, and that she'll have him without consulting her parents. The reasoning behind all this reveals a wise woman. This Gisippo, whom she's already approached, would be a pure fool to turn her down. It seems like a millennium since he started passing my shop — and that's when he began to meet with her every day. In fact, there he comes with that foreigner. Her taste isn't bad, I must admit; he's just the right sort of bed-warmer for a widow. — Have you located that friend of yours, my good man?

DEMETRIO: I've found Messer Gisippo here, the very person I was looking for.

BARBAGRIGIA: I'm glad. As a matter of fact, he's just the man I need to have a few private words with, if you'll permit us.

DEMETRIO: As you wish.

GISIPPO: No don't go. We are as one; you may bare your heart before us both.

BARBAGRIGIA: Messer Gisippo, I know others have spoken to you about the subject on my mind; now that you've

27

given it careful thought, I trust you'll be wanting to make a contract.

GISIPPO: For a wife?

BARBAGRIGIA: And what a wife! Most men who take wives might as well break their necks. But the lady I'm talking about will bring you contentment, peace and happiness. I doubt that you know who Madonna Argentina really is.

GISIPPO: If you have nothing else to say, please stop talking.

SATIRO: Master Demetrio, they're talking about the marriage. Now's the time to hammer home.

BARBAGRIGIA: But why? Are you out of your mind or isn't she a good enough match for you?

GISIPPO: Her station is far above the merits of my condition. I'm honoured to be loved and desired by a lady of her rank. I am no such friend of fortune that I can scorn her wealth. No greater opportunity could ever have been bestowed upon a man; to accept is wisdom, to refuse, folly, yet refuse I must. Destiny has cast this in my way, but only now, when I cannot avail myself of it.

BARBAGRIGIA: I can't understand you when you talk that way. Why can you not, when you want to? And you want to according to what you say yourself. My God! Here's beauty, honesty, wealth, and love rolled into one and all in a country like Rome. And you have doubts about doing it?

DEMETRIO: Perhaps you should know that Messer Gisippo here remains aloof from all women, grieving as he does in memory of his dead lady.

BARBAGRIGIA: Is it for a dead woman that you will disappoint so many living men and women and jeopardize your own future?

GISIPPO: Dead she is to the world, but in my soul she will be forever alive and immortal.

28

DEMETRIO: Even in the wisest, Messer Gisippo, the mist of
passion obscures the light of prudence. Knowing your
resolution in all things, I would not deign to counsel you
were you not caught in this very dilemma. But consider
as follows, since it is by reason that one must be
perennially ruled in the affairs of life: is it because of
grief, which is a temporary alteration of the soul, that
you will not consent to marry? Grief will pass with that
which has caused it, leaving remorse in its wake for
having missed this chance. The passage of time and the
necessities of life will soften your heart towards her, but
only after her indignation has hardened hers against
you. When she has turned away, your scorn driving her
into the arms of another, you'll yearn then for the
unattainable. Such a lady will not easily be found again.

BARBAGRIGIA: He's right. Do you think there are women
like her on every street corner?

GISIPPO: I intend no scorn in rejecting her suit; the failure
redounds solely upon myself. I remind you that the
necessities of life have no power to move those who
desire to die. As for time, I know that it is balm to many
wounds of passion, but it cannot heal my pain.

DEMETRIO: But why not?

GISIPPO: Because my pain is infinite.

DEMETRIO: This is impossible since you are finite.

GISIPPO: It is sufficient that it endures as long as I.

DEMETRIO: Your reasoning is false, since the sun never rises
without bringing some alteration both to our bodies and
our souls.

BARBAGRIGIA: You speak philosophy, but I prefer to speak
medicine. Pain inhabits the soul just as flatulence does
the body. Take this neighbour of mine, precious as
silver; make a plaster[32] of her to wrap around your heart
and you'll find yourself wondrously restored. Have you
never taken into consideration the grace and beauty of

29

that little widow? That angelic face? Those eyes of the
Holy Spirit? That figure moulded by the hands of our
Lord? How could you go on mourning, just having her
before your eyes?

GISIPPO: Alas, the memory of such beauty makes my
sorrow complete.

BARBAGRIGIA: How can this be? Is she not ravishing?

GISIPPO: I'd find her beautiful beyond compare had I never
seen Giulietta.

BARBAGRIGIA: Here we are again with Giulietta. Once you
start caring for this one, she'll seem more beautiful than
Giulietta.

DEMETRIO: It's true what he says. Experience brings love
and love brings pleasure; one nail drives out another.

GISIPPO: Mine is so driven in and riveted that even though
the shaft breaks it will never come out.

BARBAGRIGIA: You're still young, my boy. Look at this
white beard of mine; you can have faith in the simple
words of experience. I had a wife, and when she died I
thought I'd never get over it, that I'd never find such
another mate. But not much time passed before I put my
sorrow behind me and turned to my Paolina to heal my
wounds. Now I value and love her a hundred times more
than the one who died. And if she were to die today, I'd
take another tomorrow, knowing the same thing would
happen again.

GISIPPO: I could never do such a wrong to my Giulietta.

DEMETRIO: Giulietta is beyond hearing or caring about such
vanities as these; and could she hear or care, surely she
would prefer your peace, profit and honour to this
pointless grief and the damage and reproof you'll draw
with this vain faithfulness of yours. If these reasons
won't prick you then I must sting you. The blame is
yours in seeking praise for your faithfulness as a lover
while failing in your duties as a friend. Just because you

are oblivious to death, poverty and dishonour, you shouldn't condemn your friends to death or dishonour through your own fault. I feel entitled to reproach you, since your affairs are the cause of my present misery. I have lost my country, my friends and my possessions in order to gratify your heart's desire; and now with succour in view for my needs, and solace for your misery you refuse such a lady, such wealth and such a country as this noble Rome. You would not be happy for me, though I have been miserable for you. However, do as you please, and I'll seek some other compensation for my life.

SATIRO: Now he's had his back put to the wall!

GISIPPO: Messer Demetrio, it's no cause for amazement that a desperate man who has lost his own sense of right and wrong should fail to perceive the needs of a friend. I hear your words and my heart breaks, since I have been the cause of your torment and shame. Yet how can I bring myself to follow your counsel if my sorrow will not cease, if my instinct abhors it, if my dreams frighten me away from it, if the image of my love so haunts my imagination that I cannot turn my thoughts to any other woman?

DEMETRIO: I've told you that your grief will pass away, that your instincts will lead you in the right way as soon as they are free from this passion. Dreams are but dreams; images are erased by the imprint of other images.

GISIPPO: These are mere words; my heart leads me a different way.

DEMETRIO: What nonsense coming from a man of your quality. I concede that at present your affairs may seem desperate. But it is laughable to think that you are the only man alive immune to the workings of time and that for such a reason you should deprive our souls of their former privileges.

GISIPPO: Wouldn't it be the greatest betrayal in the world to accept this gentle lady, who bestows upon me her heart, her person, her wealth, if I did not love her as she deserves with all my heart?

DEMETRIO: You'll come to love her in spite of yourself. What with her conversation, her beauty, the affection she bears you, the comfort and pleasure of day to day life with her, you'll find yourself utterly transformed.

GISIPPO: And you believe that I should forget Giulietta?

DEMETRIO: Even if you don't forget her now, her memory will nevertheless wane by degrees until there is no passion left. Better to say yes while you have the chance and leave the rest to God, since it is by His design that such an opportunity has been granted to you.

GISIPPO: Oh, hallowed spirit. Look down from your abode on high. See the constancy of my soul, the depth of my grief and the strength of my longing to come to you. Hear how your name is ever on my lips; see how your image is imprinted on my heart. Know that I am yours and yours alone. Yet see also the temptations and obligations which in part move me to break my resolution. Since I have never wilfully violated the laws of love, withhold your anger now that I must perforce fulfil those of friendship. Demetrio, our dearest companion and this most faithful minister of our love, compels me to bind myself to another, though in this I do not sever my ties with you. My body is to be sold for the well-being of my friend, but my soul will ever be yours. Though I remain faithful to you, let me not be ungrateful to him. Let my few remaining days of grief on earth serve to benefit this our dear friend. And so, to release me from the torment of your absence, either call me forth to join you above, or send me, as you can, some shred of consolation. Go now Messer Demetrio; do with me as you will. My wishes are as nothing when set against my infinite debts to you.

DEMETRIO: You speak of paying a debt, and that I accept since I can prevail upon you in no other way. But I do so not for my own interest and pleasure, but for yours.

GISIPPO: My only pleasure will be in your satisfaction and the hope for a speedy death.

DEMETRIO: Would that I could furnish you daily with such risks of death!

BARBAGRIGIA: Risks! How absurd! This chap falls into a sea of happiness and thinks he's going to die. It sounds to me like the story of the nitwit who ate a whole tree full of nuts just to poison himself.[34]

DEMETRIO: Listen Barbagrigia, make sure you don't mention anything of Messer Gisippo's misery to Madonna Argentina.[35] It's enough that he's willing. Take her word to this effect and give her this jewel on his behalf. Tonight we'll place the ring on her finger.

BARBAGRIGIA: It's got to be sealed with more than a ring. It's got to be flesh into flesh this very evening.

DEMETRIO: You make sure the widow is ready and I'll look after the rest.

BARBAGRIGIA: Women are always ready. Now we're talking. I can't wait to tell her the good news!

SATIRO: Not before I get there. I want the tip for myself. There she is at the window with her maid.

NUTA: What's troubling you, Satiro?

SATIRO: A wedding! A wedding!

NUTA: Come on up! Come on up!

SCENE II   MARABEO, NUTA

MARABEO: (*alone*) I can already feel the hangman breathing down my neck; I'm sure Agatina has talked to Nuta

33

through the hole behind the stove. It seems like an age since Pilucca went to squeeze some news out of her. Oh oh, here she comes. I'd better stay out of sight.

NUTA: You're trying to hide, you dirty rascal! Marabeo! — Mistress, Marabeo doesn't want to come.

MARABEO: May the devil choke you to death, you ugly witch!

NUTA: Get upstairs, fast. The mistress wants you. We have to make arrangements for the wedding.

MARABEO: What! Wedding?

NUTA: Yes a wedding.

MARABEO: Whose?

NUTA: Our mistress's. Whose do you think?

MARABEO: No fooling? The mistress is remarrying?

NUTA: Yes, yes, remarrying.

MARABEO: The mistress is remarrying, now there's a good one. Listen, Nuta, another word.

NUTA: I told you, the mistress is waiting.

MARABEO: Nuta, darling . . .

NUTA: You've got breath to waste.

MARABEO: Listen.

NUTA: Keep your hands off me.

MARABEO: What arrogance. Well at least let me talk to you. What's this wedding you're so excited about?

NUTA: Our mistress's, haven't you got that straight yet?

MARABEO: But who with, my love?

NUTA: With her husband to be, Messer Gisippo; is that all clear now?

MARABEO: How's that? With the same Messer Gisippo who didn't want her?

NUTA: All that matters is that he wants her now. The wedding's this evening, so get upstairs.

MARABEO: What? This evening?

NUTA: Why, is it by any chance going to spoil yours with your little pussy-cat?[36]

MARABEO: What pussy-cat?

NUTA: You still deny it, you faking rascal? Haven't I seen her? Haven't I spoken to her? Hasn't she written everything to the Governor?

MARABEO: Then the Governor knows?

NUTA: He'll know the minute I give him this evidence.

MARABEO: Nuta, sweetheart, you'll be the cause of my ruin.

NUTA: What could please me more?

MARABEO: You realize that'll be the end of the nice little thing we do together?

NUTA: Humph! I've had it with your little thing.

MARABEO: I can see how you've forgotten me now that Pilucca's back.

NUTA: Neither you, nor him, nor anybody; you're all made of the same stuff, you men.

MARABEO: You should know, you've tried them all. But listen, I want the two of us to get married this evening, as well.

NUTA: You'll be married in the Pope's prison, you worthless lout.

MARABEO: Oh Nuta, sugarplum. Why so spiteful? Listen, show me what you're taking to the Governor, just for a moment.

NUTA: I'm coming, my lady, I'm coming.

35

SCENE III   MARABEO, PILUCCA

MARABEO: (*alone*) When the snow melts, that's when last
year's turds show through. Between my mistress
re-marrying and the Governor finding out that I'm
keeping this girl against her will, I'm treading on a thin
line — one way poverty, the other the gallows. Ah, here
comes Pilucca. — Well, what happened between you and
Nuta?

PILUCCA: What did you want to happen? There's a lot more
business at hand besides yours. There's business with the
poultry dealers, with the confectioners, with the cooks.

MARABEO: There's going to be a wedding, eh Pilucca?

PILUCCA: Some sort of banquet, who cares what? Pigeons,
capons, peacocks, heavy spending.

MARABEO: I didn't look for this disaster, Pilucca, not a
wedding.

PILUCCA: Such a little disaster could fill our purses and our
bellies for quite a few months.

MARABEO: There's bad luck in it for us.

PILUCCA: How come?

MARABEO: We're fine with the mistress in love, but not
married. Once she starts looking after her own yard how
can we go on scratching about? And if the husband has
a stick, how can we find out what to scratch for?

PILUCCA: Let's not worry about bad luck before it comes.
Let's enjoy this wedding first, then see what happens.

MARABEO: We should think of something before it happens.
Only the virtuous can be heedless. Half a brain is good
enough for an honest man, but for a crook even a whole
brain isn't enough. By God, I thought I'd cut off all her
routes to marriage. To think how many good catches
crossed her path and how I managed to scuttle them all.
I stoked her fires for this fellow because I knew how

36

dead set he was against marrying. I can't imagine how this sudden change came about.

PILUCCA: Well there it is. It's done now.

MARABEO: Done? By Christ, not if I can help it.

PILUCCA: What can you do about it now? The husband has already sent the wedding ring in pledge. Here I am right now preparing the dinner and all the rest; tonight's the night it's going to happen.

MARABEO: Tonight? So the fire's already put to the squib. Well, we'll launch a counter-attack, Pilucca.[37]

PILUCCA: Time's already run out.

MARABEO: We've got to make fast use of our wits. We've got to thwart them somehow, play them a foul turn, tell lies to the groom about his bride, and to the bride about her groom. Let's invent some other love affairs, make one of them an adulterer, make them both syphilitics. We can have the wedding delayed, or at least put off for this evening. Then we'll have time to devise more devilry.

PILUCCA: Make sure you don't sit down at the table after the plates are scraped clean, Marabeo.[38]

MARABEO: It's not the table I'm trying to unload, but the bed, Pilucca.

PILUCCA: Wait, I've got it. Just for laughs let's carry on with the dinner but undo everything at the same time.

MARABEO: Right, but meanwhile we can't waste chances. You see those two coming 'round the corner? The bigger one's the groom.

PILUCCA: That's Messer Gisippo?

MARABEO: That's him all right.

PILUCCA: Ah, so the other one must be Demetrio.

MARABEO: Which Demetrio?

PILUCCA: The one who escaped from jail and came to Rome
with me.

MARABEO: What's he got to do with Gisippo?

PILUCCA: How should I know? They're both levantines and
must be friends.

MARABEO: That could be to our advantage. Do you know
what I'm thinking now? That we set this Demetrio's ears
ringing with suspicions that the widow's pregnant.

PILUCCA: Good thinking.

MARABEO: In this sort of affair a little smudge blackens the
lot; a tidbit of truth and they'll swallow it all.

PILUCCA: Yes, good!

MARABEO: He doesn't know anybody else in Rome but you?

PILUCCA: Nobody else, and he doesn't realize I know
Gisippo either.

MARABEO: All the better. Looks like he's heading this way.

PILUCCA: I'll wrap him up for you in a neat little package.

MARABEO: You know who could sell the pregnancy line?
Brother Cerbone.

PILUCCA: He could turn the fiction into truth.

MARABEO: We'll worm the statement out of him in a way
that makes it sound like an act of charity.

PILUCCA: Just so, and to confirm it I'll make a kind of
confession. In the meantime, we've got to lay in provisions for the banquet.

MARABEO: Well let's get a move on; I'll carry on with the
dinner preparations while you set up the friar for snaring
Demetrio. Lure him till he falls into the trap.

PILUCCA: You think I can't manage that?

SCENE IV   MARABEO, CIULLO, LISPA, FULIGATTO

MARABEO: Ah you're just in time, Ciullo. Pick up that
    basket and follow me. Call those two rogues over here
    to help you carry this stuff.

CIULLO: Hey, Lispa, Fuligatto, zà zà.

FULIGATTO: Look there, Marabeo, somebody in the palace
    is calling you.

MARABEO: Who can that be?

LISPA: Look, he's waving at you.

MARABEO: Decked out like a sailor. There's a lot of seamen
    going around today. He looks a hell of a lot like the
    master . . . By Lucifer! It can't be him. Wait here till I
    get back.

CIULLO: We won't budge.

SCENE V   CIULLO, FULIGATTO, LISPA, MIRANDOLA

CIULLO: Let's have a hand or two to kill time.

FULIGATTO: Good idea. Get the cards out, we'll have a
    round of gilè.[39]

CIULLO: Out with the cards. The basket goes here in the
    middle, Fuligatto. Cut the deck to see who serves.

LISPA: Here comes old Mirandola. Listen, before we start,
    let's trick him into a feud with the scruffy brothers.

CIULLO: How do we do that?

LISPA: Easy. Those ragged rogues are demanding jewels
    from the Grimaldi and tonight's the time they're expect-
    ing their answer. I've been given a couple of julians[40] by
    their enemies to dupe them. All we do is convince
    Mirandola that the jewels they're demanding have been
    stolen from him.

CIULLO: Yes, perfect! Let's do it.

FULIGATTO: I'm with you.

LISPA: Fuligatto you stay there and pretend you're hearing ghosts from this cellar. I'll go down and play the ghost of the devil Malariccia. And you, Ciullo, go fetch Mirandola.

CIULLO: Don't you hear all those Mamelukes[41] down there in the cellars, Mirandola?

LISPA: Oh, Mirandola!

FULIGATTO: Listen, they're calling you.

LISPA: Oh, Mirandola!

MIRANDOLA: Who are you? Who's calling me?

LISPA: I'm Malariccia.

MIRANDOLA: What do you want with me?

LISPA: To tell you a secret.

MIRANDOLA: What secret can it be?

LISPA: Remember the Great Turk[42] who promised you a pile of gems but sent you only worthless baubles of glass?

MIRANDOLA: I remember.

LISPA: Are you acquainted with the scruffy brothers?

MIRANDOLA: Yes, I know them.

LISPA: They have stolen your jewels.

MIRANDOLA: Those damned cuckold thieves! But how could they?

LISPA: Because they are gem-cutters and the stones passed through their hands. They kept the real ones and sent fake ones to you.

MIRANDOLA: What did they do with them?

LISPA: They sold them to the Bank of St. George in Genoa, and now they're asking the Grimaldi for three thousand ducats.

MIRANDOLA: Ah, those crooked rascals. So they've decked themselves out at my expense.

LISPA: I speak for the Great Turk. Have this money of the Grimaldi's confiscated. Prepare men to undertake this enterprise.

MIRANDOLA: We must first find those who can take it away from them.

LISPA: My very reason for coming — to launch the campaign.

MIRANDOLA: With how many thousand men?

LISPA: With five thousand fifty hundred thousand.[43]

MIRANDOLA: And what is the plan of attack?

LISPA: First I place Monte Mario inside Rome.[44]

MIRANDOLA: What for?

LISPA: In order to ride on the back of Castel Sant'Angelo.

MIRANDOLA: By Jupiter, now you're catching on. Add the Colosseum and the Pantheon as gun turrets and try the columns of Trajan and Antoninus as cannons.

LISPA: And what about the spires?

MIRANDOLA: Out of the towers of St. Peter's make battering-rams, out of the others spears. The arches of the Roman baths will serve as crossbows.

LISPA: It shall be done.

MIRANDOLA: And what's that lazy Turk waiting for?

LISPA: He's waiting for Monte Mario to be put in the saddle, and for the torture poles to be sharpened.

MIRANDOLA: Why doesn't he send his Janissaries[45] in the meantime?

LISPA: He's done that too; some of them are already here in Rome.

MIRANDOLA: So where are they?

LISPA: In the chancery, drawing out money.

MIRANDOLA: So what remains to be done?

LISPA: Crown you emperor.

MIRANDOLA: Emperor of what?

LISPA: Of Testaccio.[46]

MIRANDOLA: And of Trebizond?[47]

LISPA: Of Trebizond, too.

MIRANDOLA: What are my symbols of power?

LISPA: For Testaccio this mitre [*gives him the cap of the condemned. . .*] and for Trebizond these sceptres.[48]

MIRANDOLA: These look like brooms to me.[49]

LISPA: No, no, these are the fasces of the Roman consuls.

MIRANDOLA: Doesn't Testaccio border on Picardy?[50]

LISPA: Indeed it does, and it's sure to be yours by investiture of the Count of Hangland.[51]

MIRANDOLA: Give me the sceptres.

LISPA: Here they are.

MIRANDOLA: What's this, a halter?

LISPA: No, a necklace.

MIRANDOLA: I will never starve again.

LISPA: Not if this necklace does the job.[52]

MIRANDOLA: Now I'm ready. Go fetch that gang of easterners and bring them here.

LISPA: The scruffy scoundrels will be sentenced this evening. Remember to confiscate the money.

MIRANDOLA: They'll turn it over to me in a jiffy, all nice and scented.

CIULLO, FULIGATTO, LISPA: Taràntara, taràntara, tif taf.[53]

ACT III

SCENE I

PILUCCA: (*alone*) Marabeo still hasn't showed up with the provisions. Wouldn't it be a great laugh if, in trying to stuff the mistress's belly, I lose the stuffing out of my own? Here's Demetrio. I must find out if the good friar has done his job and planted the carrot in him.[54] If he's not suspicious by now, I'll have to give it a little nudge.

SATIRO: Nincompoop! That's what happens when you marry in Rome.

PILUCCA: (*aside*) Planted it he has, indeed.

DEMETRIO: Seven years a widow, and now she's pregnant.

SATIRO: Could you just spell it out for me in plain language.

DEMETRIO: Satiro, I suspect this is a trick for stalling the marriage. Only a simpleton would credit this without further verification, but we don't have time unless we postpone the wedding and we can't do that without Gisippo. If we tell him about all this, we'll upset him and put him off the venture forever. Perhaps it's not even true. But if it is, and we don't tell him, we'd be sending him to the slaughter, his honour tainted forever. What shall we do, Satiro? We've gotten him into this labyrinth, now we have to get him out of it.

SATIRO: If you agree, we'll tell him about the pregnancy and then negotiate on our own for a delay in the nuptials, just for this evening. After that, one thing will

43

lead to another. Meanwhile, I'll search around until I get to the bottom of all this.

DEMETRIO: That's all very well, but have you got the courage to carry it through?

SATIRO: I'll try. I'll say we're not ready, that Gisippo is a bit under the weather.

DEMETRIO: Ah, here comes Pilucca. You go and take care of the wedding; I'll see what I can get out of this fellow.

PILUCCA: (*aside*) It's a cinch. He's running straight into the snare.

SCENE II   DEMETRIO, PILUCCA

DEMETRIO: Greetings, Pilucca.

PILUCCA: Oh, Messer Demetrio. Have you located that friend of yours?

DEMETRIO: Not yet. Will you help me look for him?

PILUCCA: Got too much else to do.

DEMETRIO: What kind of business are you tied up with?

PILUCCA: Wedding.

DEMETRIO: What? Don't tell me you're taking a wife?

PILUCCA: No chance. It's my mistress who's taking a husband.

DEMETRIO: She's not the one who's marrying that Greek fellow?

PILUCCA: Ah, do you know her already?

DEMETRIO: No, but I heard someone talking about her.

PILUCCA: What were they saying?

DEMETRIO: That she's a knock-out.

PILUCCA: A real knock-out.

DEMETRIO: And loaded.

PILUCCA: Really loaded.

DEMETRIO: High quality goods.

PILUCCA: Very high.

DEMETRIO: And a fairly casual companion.

PILUCCA: They went so far as to say that?[55]

DEMETRIO: And pregnant too, which is just a touch further.

PILUCCA: Pregnant?

DEMETRIO: Substantially so.

PILUCCA: Holy Mother, this is going too far. Are they really saying she's pregnant?

DEMETRIO: They're saying it all over town, which is worse.

PILUCCA: Blazes and damnation. I told her not to let that cardinal hang around.

DEMETRIO: A she-cardinal eh? But what's going to happen when the groom gets word of it?

PILUCCA: Well, if he doesn't find out before tonight, it's his tough luck.[56]

DEMETRIO: And how's it going to work out during the months to come?

PILUCCA: No problem! These days babies are produced in seven months as naturally as in nine; it's all give or take, more or less, according to one's needs.

DEMETRIO: Just listen to that.

PILUCCA: You know what I mean, eh Messer Demetrio Zoccoli?

DEMETRIO: Sure! Sure!

PILUCCA: Don't tell a soul.

DEMETRIO: Look, here comes Messer Gisippo. I must be off, Pilucca.

PILUCCA: But . . . he's the groom! Do you know him?

DEMETRIO: Eh! No matter if I do.

PILUCCA: (*aside*) Oh, what a big mouth I've got. I'll wait and see if they're friends. — Listen, Messer Demetrio, I was only kidding you just now.

DEMETRIO: Sure you were.

PILUCCA: She's not really pregnant.

DEMETRIO: She's given birth just like that?

PILUCCA: Listen to me.

DEMETRIO: Enough said. Adieu.

PILUCCA: Please.

DEMETRIO: You keep mum and so will I.

SCENE III   DEMETRIO, GISIPPO, GIOVANNI, BATTISTA
(scruffy scoundrels)

GIOVANNI: In a word, this judge is so hard-headed that no amount of reasoning will break through.

BATTISTA: There's no getting around his stubbornness.

GIOVANNI: By God, there isn't.

BATTISTA: Let's leave this business to our lawyer.[57] We'll go and have a further word with this fellow from Chios.

GIOVANNI: I'm sure he knows something about Giulietta.

BATTISTA: Ah, there he is. But who's that along with him?

GIOVANNI: I've no idea.

BATTISTA: Didn't he say he was hoping to find Tindaro in Rome? Could that be him?

GIOVANNI: We'd never recognize him; he was a mere lad when we left. But by God he certainly resembles the old man.

BATTISTA: There's a definite resemblance, all right.

GIOVANNI: Wait a minute, I know that servant.

BATTISTA: Ah, that's Satiro!

GIOVANNI: Satiro, it is!

BATTISTA: Then it's bound to be Tindaro.

GIOVANNI: It must be him, that treacherous dog.

BATTISTA: Wait, let's see if we can find out if Giulietta is in Rome.

GIOVANNI: Oh, my little girl.

BATTISTA: We can step aside here and listen in.

DEMETRIO: Messer Tindaro . . . I mean Messer Gisippo. I couldn't help saying Tindaro.

GISIPPO: As long as we're alone it doesn't matter.

DEMETRIO: Yes, but if I'm not careful, my tongue will get the best of me when there's someone else around.

GIOVANNI: Oh, the vermin. He's changed his name.

BATTISTA: He couldn't have let his tongue get the best of him at a better moment.

DEMETRIO: Are you all set for the wedding?

GISIPPO: As God wills.

DEMETRIO: You know, everything considered, I think it would be better to put it off a day or two.

GISIPPO: Would that I could put it off forever.

DEMETRIO: That's not what I meant. But to marry a Roman lady so hastily might injure her honour or even ours.

GIOVANNI: Marry a Roman lady! Then, this can't be our Giulietta.

BATTISTA: Silence a minute.

DEMETRIO: The widow would have to agree to the post-ponement.

GIOVANNI: He's taken a widow!

DEMETRIO: What shall we do?

GISIPPO: You've managed everything up to now; you can handle the rest.

DEMETRIO: All right, then. Look, I've given word that you're feeling indisposed. All you have to do is go home and feign sickness. I'll look after everything else.

GIOVANNI: Those tartars! And where have they left Giulietta?

BATTISTA: Let's go speak to them.

DEMETRIO: Wait, Messer Gisippo; I'm afraid the moment's come to render an account of Giulietta.

GISIPPO: To whom?

DEMETRIO: To her father and her uncle.

GISIPPO: Where are they?

DEMETRIO: Right here. There's no avoiding them any longer.

GISIPPO: I'm resigned, let's wait for them. Are these the ones?

DEMETRIO: These.

GISIPPO: Oh God! I feel so miserable.

DEMETRIO: That makes two of us.

GISIPPO: Messer Giovanni, I . . .

GIOVANNI: Ah, you! You've had your pleasure. Now, where is my daughter?

BATTISTA: Have you nothing to say?

GIOVANNI: Where have you left her?

BATTISTA: What have you done with her?

GIOVANNI: Can't you speak?

GISIPPO: Messer Demetrio . . .

DEMETRIO: Come now, it will all be explained in time.

GIOVANNI: What do you mean in time — when you've gone to meet your maker?

BATTISTA: Tell us something about her. Tell us you'll be faithful to her.

GIOVANNI: How is it possible? Hasn't he taken another?

GISIPPO: Oh, my grief!

DEMETRIO: Listen, let's step out of the middle of the street.

BATTISTA: Where is our Giulietta?

GISIPPO: Oh, my Giulietta.

BATTISTA: She's not dead, is she?

GISIPPO: Alas! Alas!

GIOVANNI: My girl is dead! You thief, you murderer. It wasn't enough just to abduct her. You had to kill her to take another wife. Robbery! Adultery! Murder! I'll find justice in Rome. Justice!

DEMETRIO: Cease your shouting Messer Giovanni. Messer Tindaro's only fault was in loving your daughter too much.

GIOVANNI: And that's why the poor fellow hasn't been able to take another wife?

BATTISTA: Let's not riot in the streets. Let's go straight to the Governor.

GISIPPO: What a maze I've gotten myself into.

DEMETRIO: God will help us, Messer Gisippo. Make your way home now; I must wait here for Satiro.

SCENE IV   DEMETRIO, BARBAGRIGIA, PILUCCA

DEMETRIO: (*alone*) Oh what turmoil, what desperate confusion this is. The wife he longed for is dead; the one he seeks now is pregnant. As for the first, if we flee, we will be accused of having her killed; if we stay, it will take more than words to account for her death. As for the second, if the wedding's called off we will be massacred by her relatives. On the one side lies disgrace and imprisonment, on the other strife and a cuckold's dishonour. If I tell Gisippo of the pregnancy, he'll flee and so ruin himself. If I don't tell him I betray him and leave him to his disgrace. Which alternative should I choose? Here comes Barbagrigia. It's no use; the widow won't give us time to consider.

PILUCCA: (*eavesdropping on the others*) I'd better follow Barbagrigia and find out what he's going to do about this marriage.

BARBAGRIGIA: (*unaware of the others*) She's the very fury of a woman. To pronounce widow and love is to put fire to saltpetre, coal and sulphur. By God, if this marriage doesn't come off tonight, the world will collapse back into chaos.

DEMETRIO: (*aside*) Just listen to him. All hell's broken loose today on account of us.[58]

PILUCCA: (*aside*) And for us the doors of paradise have opened wide.

BARBAGRIGIA: They say that Greeks are shrewd, but this bunch is downright insipid. They state their desires, then shilly-shally around, they make promises, then they recant. We're offering them a fortune and we have to beg them to take it. It must be true that good fortune chooses those who flee from it.

DEMETRIO: What's the matter, Barbagrigia?

BARBAGRIGIA: All the evil in the world. What are these pranks you're up to? Where's the groom?

DEMETRIO: He's sick.

BARBAGRIGIA: What kind of sickness? It's this poor lady
   who's sick and desperate because of this luckless love
   she has for him. We have to get this wedding over with
   as soon as we can.

DEMETRIO: Things aren't in order for tonight.

BARBAGRIGIA: But this would be the height of scandal.

DEMETRIO: Scandal? Why? Would you force a man to
   marry when he's sick?

BARBAGRIGIA: And would you want to disgrace this lady?

DEMETRIO: What disgrace can there be in a day's post-
   ponement?

BARBAGRIGIA: Another day? Now that all the provisions are
   bought, the relatives invited, the news yelled all over
   Rome, the house full of women and the festivities
   already begun?

DEMETRIO: I don't know. It seems to me that you shouldn't
   clamour for something you can't get. An accident
   shouldn't be taken for an insult.

BARBAGRIGIA: But surely something can be done if you try!
   I'm warning you: when honour's at stake these Romans
   are very fussy. This smells more like a retreat than a
   postponement if you ask me. And if that's so, you'd be
   advised to reconsider. My faith has been pledged. I've
   presented the ring on your behalf, and on your behalf
   the wedding has been proclaimed. Now if the event
   doesn't take place, there will be a huge scandal. A
   woman's rage knows no bounds, and this is a lady of
   power and influence, as you know. May I simply remind
   you to look well to your friend's honour and your own
   debts.

DEMETRIO: Is it a criminal act to be sick?

BARBAGRIGIA: This evening he'll feel better. Let's go. I want
   to speak to him.

DEMETRIO: He's resting right now. You go present his apologies while I call for the doctor.

BARBAGRIGIA: I haven't the courage to face her. I'm going to look after my own affairs; you can arrange it among yourselves.

PILUCCA: (*aside*) Oh bless you! Nobody could have spoiled this marriage better than you, not even the marriage contract wrecker himself.

DEMETRIO: Here come the Canali; they've been to see the Governor. Let's not stay around here; we might find ourselves tangling with some evil spirits.

SCENE V   ATTORNEY AT LAW, MIRANDOLA, GIOVANNI, BATTISTA (scruffy scoundrels)

ATTORNEY: Most certainly you can have him seized and made to answer for your daughter. Every kind of lawsuit in the world is known in the tribunals of Rome. Let's go to the Governor and I'll get you a warrant for his arrest.[59]

MIRANDOLA: Hey there, doctor, you with the gown on.

ATTORNEY: What's the matter, Mirandola?

MIRANDOLA: Aren't you the attorney of these ragged brothers?

ATTORNEY: I am indeed.

MIRANDOLA: I must tell you, then, that the jewels they are disputing with the Grimaldi belong to me.

ATTORNEY: What do you mean, to you?

MIRANDOLA: They are mine, and these two have stolen them from me.

ATTORNEY: How did you find this out?

MIRANDOLA: The ghost of Malariccia has revealed it to me.

ATTORNEY: If so you've got it from the right source. Go talk to them about it (*indicating the brothers*).

MIRANDOLA: You bloody thieves! You swindlers!

BATTISTA: What, us thieves?

GIOVANNI: Us swindlers?

MIRANDOLA: Yes, you; I want either my jewels back or the money from the Grimaldi.

GIOVANNI: Who are you to level such accusations?

MIRANDOLA: I am myself. Today, Mirandola, tomorrow someone else who'll have you hung, you rats.

BATTISTA: You must be somebody else already to offer such inanities.

GIOVANNI: You must be crazy.

MIRANDOLA: And you must be wicked robbers. Haven't I got the letter from the Great Turk saying that he's sending me these jewels? Here it is right here, and the inventory as well.

BATTISTA: And here is our inventory.

ATTORNEY: Aha! Let's see if they're the same. You read out yours and I'll read Mirandola's.

BATTISTA: "List of the jewels that are sold by us, Giovanni and Battista Canali, to Saint George of Genoa as ornaments for the statue of the saint."

ATTORNEY: "List of the jewels that the Great Turk sends as a gift to Mirandola for his coronation."[60]

BATTISTA: First of all "a huge pointed diamond of one ounce, set into the iron of his spear."

ATTORNEY: "A pointed diamond of one ounce which was the tip of the helmet of the Caliph Timer Lung."[61]

BATTISTA: "Two big topaz stones cut as bosses for his horse."

ATTORNEY: "Two cobble-sized topaz stones, set as pater-nosters for the bit of Bucephallus."[62]

BATTISTA: "Sixteen-pointed diamonds for the rowels of his spurs."

ATTORNEY: "Sixteen-pointed diamonds, which were the knots in the club of Salah-ed-din."[63]

BATTISTA: "A balas of two ounces fixed in the breast plate of his armour."

ATTORNEY: "A balas of two ounces, which was a button from the belt of Mohammed."

BATTISTA: "A brooch of rubies, emeralds, diamonds and sapphires used as the young girl's earring."

ATTORNEY: This item as well, "which belonged to the Empress of Orbec."[64]

BATTISTA: "And two rubies for the eyes of the dragon."[65]

ATTORNEY: Here they are, "which belonged to the head of Medusa."

BATTISTA: Is there "the ruby spinel of seventy carats?"

ATTORNEY: Yes, "the ruby spinel of seventy carats."

BATTISTA: And "the sword handle of jasper?"

ATTORNEY: "The handle of jasper from the very sword of Aeneas." Ah, these all match together.

MIRANDOLA: You see what these scoundrels have wrenched from me?

ATTORNEY: So what are your intentions?

GIOVANNI: Tobias[66] himself couldn't have bettered such idle fancies as these.

BATTISTA: He's talking utter nonsense.

MIRANDOLA: You'll know my intentions when we go before the Governor.

ATTORNEY: Then let's go to him.

MIRANDOLA: If he doesn't support my view, I'll support it with my own hands. Just wait till you see what's simmering in the pot for you.

ACT IV

SCENE I   MARABEO. PILUCCA

MARABEO: (*alone*) Where in God's name has my master come from, and on this of all days? That knave Pilucca must have betrayed me. I'll bet they came back together. I'll bet the master sent Pilucca ahead with news of his death to search his wife's soul and sample the humours of the household. If it's true, then I've gnawed the bait in the trap. But before you'll get me, my dear Pilucca and my scheming master, I'll make you suffer so horribly that God alone knows how you'll come out of it.

PILUCCA: (*aside*) He's in a fit of anger; he must not realize how well things are going. — Marabeo, it looks like our lady will be without her spouse, after all.

MARABEO: The other one she'll find in his place will be a lot worse for her and for us.

PILUCCA: Which other one?

MARABEO: You're asking me that, you package of misery? Don't forget you've tried to have me sacked once already.

PILUCCA: What's this you're raving about?

MARABEO: I'm looking at a face ready to lie. Now answer me this: you've returned with the master haven't you?

PILUCCA: With which master?

MARABEO: With which? With the Cavaliere Jordano.

PILUCCA: What's this you say? Is he still alive?

56

MARABEO: As alive as you should be dead.

PILUCCA: He's back?

MARABEO: You ought to know, you bastard.

PILUCCA: The master's back?

MARABEO: You bet it's the master. Didn't you come with him?

PILUCCA: Not me.

MARABEO: So you've decided to uncover my frauds, but don't forget what I know of yours.

PILUCCA: I haven't a clue what you're screeching about, Marabeo.

MARABEO: What a two-bit doublecrosser you are.

PILUCCA: Think what you like, I don't know anything about it.

MARABEO: Either you're lying, or fortune is playing us some dirty tricks.

PILUCCA: Anything is possible, except that I've betrayed you.

MARABEO: But you told me the master was dead.

PILUCCA: So I did, and I believed it too. It was never certain, but I was fed up with having to go on looking for him.

MARABEO: And what are your hopes of saving yourself, now that he's back?

PILUCCA: I'll come up with excuses, just as I did then. I'll say it was told to me in such a place, at such a time, by such a person so don't blame me, blame him.

MARABEO: Then you know nothing about it?

PILUCCA: Nothing.

MARABEO: And you haven't come with him?

PILUCCA: How many times do I have to tell you?

MARABEO: That's amazing! What's happening, anyway? The dead are resurrected, the lost are found again. Both were prisoners of the Moors, both came back from the sea after years, the one not knowing about the other, and all on the same day. One fills here while the other pours there. What the hell is going on today?

PILUCCA: The master has really returned?

MARABEO: You'll see.

PILUCCA: Where is he?

MARABEO: At my place.

PILUCCA: How did he get there?

MARABEO: Once freed by the galleys of the Pope, he made for the Piazza Farnese, but he couldn't find his house. Not wanting to be seen in his derelict condition he came to my house, which he got into through the back door, in order to make himself more presentable.

PILUCCA: His homecoming will be universally unwelcomed. Does he know that the mistress is about to remarry?

MARABEO: He knows that and a lot of other things I told him too. Dare I trust you, Pilucca?

PILUCCA: You ask me that, Marabeo? I have as much at stake in this as you do, you know.

MARABEO: Now that the master's here, it's not enough to have obstructed the mistress' wedding with Gisippo. If that was a cancer, this is a plague. You've spread false reports of his death, I've robbed him blind, and before you left your hands weren't always in your pockets. Now his wife has shamed him and he's raging mad. He's desperate. The mothers who spawned us are pitiful whores if we don't find a way to wipe him out.

PILUCCA: You scare me stiff.

MARABEO: I'm shaking all over myself.

PILUCCA: What are we going to do, then?

MARABEO: There are two ways of taking care of him: get
    him into a showdown with Gisippo or a war with the
    mistress. Gisippo might snuff him out at once; failing
    that, the mistress could make his life hell for years to
    come. I've been working on both routes. I told him how
    the mistress welcomed his death, how she longed to
    marry Gisippo and that the union had been planned for
    this very night. That's put the very devil into him. I've
    reminded him how easily he can avenge himself since
    everyone takes him for dead and no one knows of his
    return. One way or the other, Cain over Abel or Abel
    over Cain, one of them will remain dead, the other will
    disappear, and we'll be free of them both forever.

PILUCCA: But do we want to risk damnation for it?

MARABEO: Let the world fall into ruin so long as we come
    out on top. Either we put no limits on our wickedness,
    or we stop meddling right now.

PILUCCA: So how do we arrange this showdown?

MARABEO: No problem there, but we've got a long way to
    go before we're ready for that. By the way, since we're
    risking our lives anyway, we might as well take the
    opportunity to pick up a hundred scudi in the business.

PILUCCA: Not even an alchemist can get gold out of risking
    his life.

MARABEO: Here's how. You know what they could do to
    me for keeping that girl by force. Listen, not only has
    the master seen her, but he's fallen in love with her, even
    though he's frothing at the mouth after Gisippo. He
    wants to buy her from me at virtually any price. He's
    planning to massacre Gisippo and take her away. So, if I
    can't get the most, I'm willing to settle for the least.

PILUCCA: Not bad.

MARABEO: Meanwhile, if the Governor finds out about it,
    he'll be sending for her, and me too, which is worse. So
    I'll have to lie low for a while and get her out of the
    house.

PILUCCA: Where can we stash her away?

MARABEO: Brother Cerbone harbours all the rest of our
contraband.

PILUCCA: A great idea, but how will we manage without her
being seen?

MARABEO: My place is just here in front, as you know.
We'll wait for the right moment, then bundle her off to
another hiding place.

PILUCCA: Seems a good plan.

MARABEO: Oh look, there's that beast of a master, too
impatient to wait at home while we set up Gisippo. I'm
going to give orders to have the girl transferred. You go
deal with the master, and if Gisippo happens along
make sure you point him out, and pretend to help the
master against him. That's sure to bring them into
combat.

PILUCCA: Right you are, but I'm afraid to approach him;
look how he hurls himself around.

MARABEO: Just the mention of Agata will calm him down.

SCENE II   JORDANO, PILUCCA

JORDANO: (*alone*) This wedding tonight's going to turn into
a funeral. I can feel it. If I catch sight of him I'll pounce
on him then and there. I could tear open his rib cage
and eat his heart.

PILUCCA: (*aside*) I feel like my guts are in a bowl.

JORDANO: (*aside*) By his livery this fellow must be one of
his menage.

PILUCCA: Sir, its me sir, Pilucca, one of yours; don't beat
me.

JORDANO: You're dressed as a galley slave.

PILUCCA: It's for your sake that I've been prisoner in the galleys. Oh master, I've been searching for you everywhere, and I'm so happy . . .

JORDANO: Go to hell. Is this the time for salutations? Where's the groom? Let me get a look at him. The anger and shame is killing me, just to know he's alive.

PILUCCA: Have patience. He's bound to come along.

JORDANO: Where's Marabeo?

PILUCCA: He's gone to move Agatina for you.

JORDANO: There's that headache too; I'm also in love.

PILUCCA: Oh, there's no greater danger in the world.

JORDANO: How can it be possible that love can be born into a breast charged with anger and vengeance?

PILUCCA: (*aside*) His mind's beginning to wander, — Master!

JORDANO: How great a tyrant over men is beauty, and how young and ravishing is this girl.

PILUCCA: (*aside*) He's put off the lion's skin for the lamb's.

JORDANO: Love and cruelty have besieged me at once.

PILUCCA: (*aside*) By God, it's verse. Now for the lute and a little sighing.

JORDANO: Ah, me!

PILUCCA: (*aside*) Just as I said. This plot of ours will go right up his fundament.

JORDANO: What's that you say, Pilucca?

PILUCCA: I was saying that your enemy will soon be in your pocket and your girlfriend in your breeches.

JORDANO: You rogue. You're making light of me?

PILUCCA: I'm telling the truth; she's at your disposal.

JORDANO: It's easy for you to say.

PILUCCA: She's in your power.

JORDANO: Only her body.

PILUCCA: What else do you want from her?

JORDANO: Her soul.

PILUCCA: Damn it, you want her breath too? You want her dead?

JORDANO: Dead she'd be to me if I had only her body.

PILUCCA: Let's hear it for spiritual love. Look — if you can have your pleasure, what else do you want?

JORDANO: Now you speak like the beast you are.

PILUCCA: Have you tried wooing her?

JORDANO: In a thousand ways. I've tried flattery and beggary, promises and gifts. I've wept, shown my anger and threatened. What haven't I done? I even went to her — dagger in hand — like Tarquinius.[67] But to no avail. She'd rather die than consent.

PILUCCA: Have patience. It takes time for the grain to ripen. Oh, master, master, look. It's Gisippo walking over there along the via Giulia.

JORDANO: Which one is he?

PILUCCA: That's him on the right. He's not alone, master. I'd better draw my weapon too.

JORDANO: Let there be a hundred with him; I'll kill and kill till my wrath is satisfied.

PILUCCA: Then you won't be needing me and I won't stand in your way. Charge them while I cut them off in front.

SCENE III   PILUCCA, MARABEO, AGATINA, ATTORNEY

PILUCCA: (aside) I'd better get moving. I may be the one who has to prepare the egg whites for the bruises. Oh, there's Marabeo at the door.

MARABEO: Well, Pilucca, what have you managed to get done?

PILUCCA: I've spread rabies amongst the dogs.

MARABEO: Well, leave them to rip the hides off each other. Help me to get this girl out of the house.

PILUCCA: Can we manage it without any noise?

MARABEO: I think so. She's been so besieged by the master, she came to me, herself, and asked to be taken away for fear of further battle with him. She promised to come willingly. Brother Cerbone is already waiting for us. Let's keep her here behind the door until the way is clear. Meanwhile, you make a quick check around. Come down here.

PILUCCA: The road's clear. Let's go.

MARABEO: Now, come on.

PILUCCA: Wow, a real firecracker.

MARABEO: You're dragging your feet.

AGATINA: Oh Blessed Virgin help me!

MARABEO: Hey, didn't you promise to come along willingly?

AGATINA: Yes, but only this far, you thugs. Now, may the heavens be witness of the violence you've used against me. Help, good people, help!

MARABEO: May God help us!

AGATINA: Help!

MARABEO: Let's gag her Pilucca.

AGATINA: Oh! Oh! Oh!

PILUCCA: Yelp all you want. This way, I said, this way.

MARABEO: We're in trouble. The Attorney's come to the window.

PILUCCA: This girl will be our ruin.

ATTORNEY: What insolence is this?

AGATINA: Oh! Oh! Oh!

ATTORNEY: Where are you dragging that girl?

MARABEO: Pull her, will you.

PILUCCA: You push her.

ATTORNEY: Do you hear me? This is an ugly looking
business. Neighbours! Neighbours! Look to the street.
My gown, give me my gown.

MARABEO: What are we going to do, Pilucca?

PILUCCA: How should I know?

MARABEO: I'll turn her loose and you take her.

PILUCCA: Sure, I'm just dying to be hanged in your place.

MARABEO: I'm getting out of here.

PILUCCA: So am I. Let's beat it.

SCENE IV   AGATINA, ATTORNEY

AGATINA: What an outrage this is! What cruelty! Is it
possible that one can find neither mercy nor justice in
Rome? Even as a prisoner of the Turks my honour was
spared, but here among Christians, I'm subjected to
violent assault and martyrdom. Oh my Tindaro, where
are you? If only you knew where I am.

ATTORNEY: What's the cause of this turmoil, my child?

AGATINA: Oh my lord, for the love of God, don't let them
dishonour me so.

ATTORNEY: Who is tormenting you?

AGATINA: A cruel brute, a certain Marabeo, who lives in
this house and who has kept me for months against my
will. These irons and these bruises are a testimony of the

tortures he has inflicted upon my body in order first to
rob me of my virginity, then offer me for sale.

ATTORNEY: He's a felon worthy of the gallows. To think of
such assaults on a virgin, in Rome, in the Piazza
Farnese, in the time of Paul III and with the Pope here,
now, in this very palace. But you're safe now, my child,
don't worry. This villain will be punished.

AGATINA: Is the Pope here indeed? Oh my lord, if you could
only bring me to the feet of His Holiness you would
hear wondrous things, for I was freed from the Turks by
his galleys. To think of it. This base born slave has
dared to deprive me of my freedom, the freedom that I
received as a gift from the loftiest of princes! The glory
due His Holiness for his noble deed has never been
revealed because of this incarceration of my body.

ATTORNEY: This is beyond all doubt a meritorious case and
worthy of pity. Leave it in my hands, my daughter, and
I promise you satisfaction. Meanwhile, here is the house
of a Roman lady who'll make you feel entirely at home.
I have an appointment now with certain of my clients.
Their problems will require only a bit of my time, then
I'll come right back to hear your case and offer my help.
(*To a maid standing by*) You take her in and, on my
behalf, request of Madonna Argentina to give her shelter
and not let her leave the house till I've spoken with her.

SCENE V   ATTORNEY, GIOVANNI, BATTISTA (scruffy
scoundrels), MIRANDOLA

ATTORNEY: (*aside*) The audacity of the wicked amazes me.
Consider the hazards they run in committing such deeds
under the very eyes of our wise and lofty prince.

BATTISTA: Oh, here comes our attorney.

ATTORNEY: If I haven't done a turn for you today never call me attorney again. I was just going inside to wait for you.

BATTISTA: Have you obtained the warrant against Tindaro?

ATTORNEY: Not only that, but I've instructed the Captain of the Guards to act on it some time ago.

BATTISTA: What else have you done for us?

ATTORNEY: What more can you want than to see an end to all this litigation?

GIOVANNI: Did we get a favourable decree?

ATTORNEY: Favourable.

GIOVANNI: God be praised. You're a worthy man, Messer Rossello.

BATTISTA: Well done, Messer Rossello. But what was Mirandola's claim all about?

ATTORNEY: Mirandola's a lunatic. That list was concocted by our enemies in order to confound tonight's settlement. But although the decree is in our favour, this leech will not drop off without a little help from us. And because his mind runs on jewels and spirits, I've got a trick in mind. Look, over there. He's coming and looking hungry as hell's mouth. Have you got a glass bead on you or some stone to show him?

BATTISTA: Here's a cheap ring.

ATTORNEY: Perfect. You keep it and I'll do the talking. Just agree to everything I say.

MIRANDOLA: What a damned fool decree. Have it your own way with your decree, but I'll have my jewels. If not, by the weeping Virgin's body, I'll have you put in a press. I'll have the essence of dirt squeezed out of you both.

ATTORNEY: Come over here Mirandola; let's settle this matter right now.

MIRANDOLA: Just give me my jewels.

ATTORNEY: How, if they don't have them?

MIRANDOLA: Then give me money.

ATTORNEY: They have none.

MIRANDOLA: Then what's the bargain you want to make?

ATTORNEY: To give you other jewels equal in value or
    greater in virtue. What more could you want than the
    bloodstone of Calandrino?[68]

MIRANDOLA: Calandrino who? But I might agree if they had
    the ring of Angelica.[69]

ATTORNEY: They have that too.

MIRANDOLA: The one that makes people invisible?

ATTORNEY: The very one.

MIRANDOLA: But I see them.

ATTORNEY: Because they haven't put it in their mouth.

MIRANDOLA: If you give me that one, I'll be satisfied.

BATTISTA: But we won't be.

ATTORNEY: Well, just let him see it.

GIOVANNI: Here it is.

MIRANDOLA: Let me just hold it for a moment.

GIOVANNI: Well, I don't know about that.

MIRANDOLA: Why not?

ATTORNEY: Because you'd put it in your mouth and
    disappear.

MIRANDOLA: (aside) If only I could have it. — Why don't
    you hold it and put just a little of it in my mouth?

ATTORNEY: All right, let's try it then.

MIRANDOLA: Can you still see me?

ATTORNEY: Oh, this is amazing. I can see only half of you
    Mirandola, only one side.

MIRANDOLA: Why are you hitting me?

ATTORNEY: I'm trying to touch you to see if the other side is still there. You only have one eye; where is the other one?

MIRANDOLA: You're tearing it out.

ATTORNEY: I can still feel you this way, but I can't see you.

MIRANDOLA: Much more of that and I won't be able to see you either.

ATTORNEY: Now put the ring right into his mouth and see if he disappears completely. Go on, don't worry. It's incredible. Now I don't see you at all.

MIRANDOLA: Uh! Uh!

GIOVANNI: Not so tight with your teeth, Mirandola. Ouch, ouch, you're biting me.

ATTORNEY: Mirandola, you blackguard! Hold on tight, don't let him get the ring away.

GIOVANNI: A curse, he's biting my finger off. Ouch! Ouch!

BATTISTA: Has he gotten it away from you?

GIOVANNI: Oh, my finger!

BATTISTA: Oh, the ring!

MIRANDOLA: You fools, I've tricked you.

ATTORNEY: This is pure treachery, Mirandola.

MIRANDOLA: To hell with the whole pack of you. Should I let such a lucky break slip past me?

BATTISTA: Oh, Mirandola!

GIOVANNI: Mirandola!

MIRANDOLA: Follow me, come on. Now that I'm invisible, the whole world is mine.

GIOVANNI: Here he is over here, no over there.

BATTISTA: Over there? No, over here.

MIRANDOLA: You can search to your heart's content.

ATTORNEY: Ha, ha, ha. He's on his way. Ha, ha, ha. That's the end of all your litigation. We've gotten rid of the madman, and he thinks he's happy to boot.

BATTISTA: We'd be happy too but for one thing: we've regained our possessions, but we've lost our own flesh and blood.

ATTORNEY: Your daughter I can't bring back to life, but I vow that this Gisippo will answer for her death. You go and hasten the serving of the warrant. I have another important matter to attend to at Madonna Argentina's house.

ACT V

SCENE I BARBAGRIGIA, ARGENTINA

BARBAGRIGIA: (*alone*) Nothing so strange as this has happened in a long time. This poor neighbour of mine must be desperate. I should try and comfort her and get her out of the house so that beast of a Cavaliere won't be able to torment her. Ah, there she is at the door; she must have sent the maids away. — Cheer up, Madonna. For everything there is a remedy.

ARGENTINA: A remedy? Only by casting myself in the river can I wash away the shame Gisippo has brought me today.

BARBAGRIGIA: It was all for the best; if things had continued there would have been a greater mess, now that our patron is back.

ARGENTINA: Which patron?

BARBAGRIGIA: You don't know? Our patron, the Cavaliere.

ARGENTINA: My husband Jordano has returned?

BARBAGRIGIA: Returned — yes!

ARGENTINA: Jesus! Jesus! So he's not dead?

BARBAGRIGIA: Dead? Well, if he is, he's trying to make a few others dead along with him.

ARGENTINA: What do you mean?

BARBAGRIGIA: He's been trying to kill Gisippo.

ARGENTINA: Where has he come from today, this man?

BARBAGRIGIA: He was in such a fit of rage I didn't ask.

70

They were fighting, and Gisippo had the upper hand. Just when he was about to kill him, the papal guard arrived and separated them. Now I don't know where they've gone.

ARGENTINA: What a dangerous and shameful situation I'm in. How long I waited for him, how long I had him sought after, how many testimonies I've had of his death, yet how slow I've been in seeking a new alliance. And now that Pilucca brings proof of his death and I, at last, decide to remarry, the fiancé I've taken doesn't want me and my dead husband comes back to life. A short time ago I was a widow. Now I'm twice married and the wife of none. Surely this is a new and unheard of misfortune.

BARBAGRIGIA: God will help you, Madonna. But while the Cavaliere is in his fit of anger, you'd best not stay here. Come with me and I'll look after you as well as a good friend and neighbour can.

ARGENTINA: There's no need, for I have nothing to fear from him. It's not guilt that troubles me — it's shame.

BARBAGRIGIA: Then there's nothing to worry about. You go back inside and I'll stay here to see what develops.

SCENE II   DEMETRIO. BARBAGRIGIA. GISIPPO. SATIRO

DEMETRIO: First our lives are in danger, and now we're under threat of arrest. Let's flee before the Canali have us seized. Wait, here's Barbagrigia.

BARBAGRIGIA: Oh, Messer Gisippo, are you wounded?

GISIPPO: No, no.

BARBAGRIGIA: And you, Messer Demetrio?

DEMETRIO: Me neither.

BARBAGRIGIA: Thank God for that. I've never seen anything like this in all my life.

GISIPPO: Who was that who tried to murder us?

BARBAGRIGIA: A man already dead himself.

DEMETRIO: Strange corpses one finds in this city.

BARBAGRIGIA: That was the husband of your wife.

DEMETRIO: Now there's a good one! Husband of the wife of another man.

BARBAGRIGIA: It's the widow's husband.

DEMETRIO: Here the widows are married!

GISIPPO: You make me laugh in spite of myself.

BARBAGRIGIA: I can see now it must sound like nonsense to you. I'll try to be clearer. That was the dead Cavaliere Jordano.

DEMETRIO: He's alive . . .

BARBAGRIGIA: . . . Who was the husband . . .

DEMETRIO: . . . Who is the husband . . .

BARBAGRIGIA: . . . Of Madonna Argentina, who was a widow . . .

DEMETRIO: . . . Who is married.

BARBAGRIGIA: . . . To you . . .

DEMETRIO: . . . To him . . .

BARBAGRIGIA: Whom does she belong to — him, you, both or neither of you? What's to happen now? I can't tell because I don't understand it and so I babble senselessly about it, because it makes no sense to me and . . .

DEMETRIO: Stop, we understand you. That was her husband, believed dead, but now alive. He came back, and when he found out that Gisippo wanted his wife he wanted Gisippo's life.

BARBAGRIGIA: Yes, sir. Amongst us all we've managed to

unravel the whole mess, but only in words. How will we untangle the situation itself?

DEMETRIO: Here comes Satiro looking frightened; he must have heard about the attack by the Cavaliere. Don't fret Satiro, we've suffered no harm.

SATIRO: Good lord, what is this if not the resurrection of the dead?

DEMETRIO: Never mind. We'll see to it that he dies again, only this time for good.

SATIRO: Who do you want to die?

DEMETRIO: Why, Cavaliere Jordano. Isn't that who you're talking about?

SATIRO: What Cavaliere Jordano? Giulietta has risen from the dead, Giulietta!

GISIPPO: Giulietta who, you donkey?

SATIRO: You'll never believe what I've seen, Master.

GISIPPO: You've seen some ghost or other?

SATIRO: I've seen her. I've seen Giulietta, and with these very eyes.

GISIPPO: Someone who looks like her, perhaps?

SATIRO: She herself.

GISIPPO: Giulietta?

SATIRO: Giulietta.

GISIPPO: My Giulietta?

SATIRO: Yours.

GISIPPO: Alive?

SATIRO: Alive.

GISIPPO: Where?

SATIRO: In the house of Madonna Argentina.

GISIPPO: Are you in your right mind?

SATIRO: I haven't been drinking, I'm not stark raving mad, I'm not dreaming. I've seen her. I've spoken to her and she has spoken to me, and here — she gave me something — this letter and this ring.

DEMETRIO: This is the day of marvels.

BARBAGRIGIA: It's doomsday if you ask me.

DEMETRIO: If this is true! Think what would have happened! What a catastrophe! Two husbands of one wife and two wives of one husband under the same roof.

GISIPPO: My God! This is the very ring I wedded her with, and this is a letter from her.

DEMETRIO: Didn't you tell me she's dead?

GISIPPO: So I thought, alas.

DEMETRIO: And this ring?

GISIPPO: It is hers.

DEMETRIO: And this letter?

GISIPPO: It's in her handwriting.

DEMETRIO: How can this be? Let me read it. "Tindaro, my master, for so I must call you now that I find myself servant to the servants in the house of your betrothed. What infinite misfortune I have endured, and all with patience in the hope of finding you, my husband and my consolation. But now that I have found you at last, you have been taken from me. Hopeless and in despair, I long only for death . . ."[70]

GISIPPO: Alas, what words are these? Read on.

DEMETRIO: "Oh Tindaro, you are taking another, yet are you not my husband? Though our union is unconsummated and though your love for me is gone, yet by this ring you are mine and owe me the duty of those vows. Did I not, contrary to my wishes, abandon my poor mother and journey far from my beloved country in order to be your wife? Remember that it was for you that I endured so many tempests and fell prey to pirates.

For you I became as one already dead, for you I was sold, imprisoned and beaten. Though you have allied yourself with another, I have resisted all advances; through so many harsh and cruel misfortunes I have remained constant to you both in body and in soul. Will you, who are under no constraints, who have been neither beaten nor sold, remarry of your own free will?"

GISIPPO: Giulietta writes these things?

DEMETRIO: "Only death can free me from this present sorrow, yet I would not die reviled and a slave. In order to remove all doubts I shall present myself to my family with a witness of my virginity to prove that I followed you not for wantonness, but for true love. As for my present state, if my prayers have any power to touch you, let me not die as the slave of another, though I cannot die as your beloved. I beg you either to employ legal means to secure my release or entreat your betrothed to free me. Surely so gentle a lady will concede to your wishes. Offer her the full sum that was paid for me; you have my promise that you will be repaid . . ."

GISIPPO: Oh the grief that cries out from these pages.

DEMETRIO: "Your refusal can but precipitate my death, which I desire as much to end my misery as to remove myself as an obstruction to your future happiness. As proof of my good will, I return to you the wedding ring you gave me, though my love for you will never wane. May health be yours and joy at your nuptials. From the house of your bride. The wretched Giulietta."

GISIPPO: Is it from the underworld, Satiro, that you have brought these words, or is it a monstrous trick?

SATIRO: I tell you, Giulietta is alive. These things come directly from her.

GISIPPO: Either what I am hearing now is a dream, or what I saw was an illusion. My soul is besieged with a myriad passions: I burn, I tremble, I marvel, I'm incredulous, I rejoice, I'm saddened, I'm ashamed! We saw her die, Satiro, and if she is dead, how has this resurrection come about? And if she is not dead, who was the one we saw slain?[71]

SATIRO: She explained all that to me too, how she was placed on the ship's stern, how another woman was killed in her stead, and how they were later overtaken by the galleys of the Pope. Suffice it to say that after many adventures, she finds herself now, under the name of Agatina, forcefully kept by Madonna Argentina's steward.

DEMETRIO: And how did she learn about Tindaro, since he also changed his name?

SATIRO: The ring you bestowed upon Madonna Argentina was the clue. Then she saw me and I clarified everything for her.

GISIPPO: Oh my beloved Giulietta!

DEMETRIO: Where are you going?

GISIPPO: To see her.

DEMETRIO: Take care. Have you forgotten? Consider the enmity between you and the Cavaliere.

GISIPPO: You consider it. You're the one who got me into this mess.

DEMETRIO: I got you into it for your own good. But then good advice and the final results are not born in the same moment. I counselled you well enough; it was you who made a bad resolution to marry. If you tell me that Giulietta is dead, should I expect her to come back to life?

GISIPPO: None of this matters now; just help me find a remedy, for I can think of nothing but her.

DEMETRIO: In sending back your lady and the husband of Madonna Argentina at the same time, fortune herself has given us the means to turn the whole household topsy turvy. This affair will virtually take care of itself. All we have to do is protect ourselves from the wrath of the Cavaliere. We'll send Barbagrigia to Madonna Argentina and Satiro to Giulietta.

BARBAGRIGIA: Why should I be any longer concerned with this neighbour of mine?

DEMETRIO: You must explain what you've heard and seen, but nothing else for now.

SATIRO: Or I with Giulietta?

DEMETRIO: You'll take her a letter from your master and console her at the same time. You can do it easily since you know everything that has happened. You go home, Messer Gisippo, and take Satiro with you. Write the letter and send it off.

GISIPPO: How can I wait so long before seeing her?

DEMETRIO: Well, I don't know.

GISIPPO: What do you want me to write, that I'm out of my mind?

DEMETRIO: Love will dictate the answer and Satiro will deliver it. Enough of this. Look the Canali are coming this way to have us arrested. God speed. I'll look after this matter. And you, Barbagrigia, do as I told you.

SCENE III   GIOVANNI, BATTISTA (scruffy scoundrels), DEMETRIO, ATTORNEY

GIOVANNI: Tindaro must be around here; there's his companion.

BATTISTA: The Captain of the Guards is probably in the Campo di Fiore. Let's go fetch him.

DEMETRIO: Hold off, Messer Battista. We can account for Giulietta without the Captain of the Guards.

BATTISTA: What's there to account for if she's dead?

DEMETRIO: But Giulietta's not dead; we only thought she was. She's alive.

GIOVANNI: You're stalling for time.

DEMETRIO: I'm giving you the honest truth.

GIOVANNI: Where is she?

DEMETRIO: You'll find out later.

BATTISTA: It can't be true.

DEMETRIO: I tell you she's alive and safe; would that she were happy as well.

GIOVANNI: About what?

DEMETRIO: About her Tindaro.

BATTISTA: And how can we make her happy about Tindaro if he has taken another wife?

DEMETRIO: If you give your consent, his wife will be Giulietta.

GIOVANNI: How on earth? Will he marry two at once?

DEMETRIO: He'll marry her alone — that is, if you'll permit it.

BATTISTA: How is this possible?

DEMETRIO: It will be so — you'll see.

GIOVANNI: If it can be done. If she is not dead . . .

DEMETRIO: Tell me that you'll accept such a marriage.

GIOVANNI: We will.

DEMETRIO: Now I can reveal myself to you as Demetrio and rejoice with you in this general happiness.

GIOVANNI: Ah, Demetrio!

BATTISTA: Ah, Demetrio! We . . .

DEMETRIO: Please, no recriminations right now. What I have done was done for the best. Accept it as such and all will be well.

GIOVANNI: Giulietta is alive?

DEMETRIO: She is alive.

GIOVANNI: Where is she?

DEMETRIO: In Rome.

GIOVANNI: But where in Rome?

DEMETRIO: In this very house.

BATTISTA: Here comes the attorney all brimful of smiles.

GIOVANNI: What's the good news, Messer Rossello?

ATTORNEY: Everything that is needed to make your joy
complete: your daughter is alive. I've done for you the
service of recovering her, together with your belongings.

BATTISTA: Oh Messer Rossello, is it really true?

GIOVANNI: Oh, beloved Giulietta!

BATTISTA: What destiny brought her to your hands?

ATTORNEY: Destiny it was indeed. I chanced to meet that
wretched Marabeo with a friend dragging her by force,
as I found out from her, into the grasp of the Cavaliere
Jordano.

DEMETRIO: The Cavaliere Jordano? This is a veritable wife
market.

GIOVANNI: What is it you're saying about my daughter?

ATTORNEY: Never mind now. She's been freed and placed in
this household. I questioned her and confirmed that she
is your daughter. She then told me everything that
happened to her. I have undertaken to see that her
freedom is secure, and I intend to see these scoundrels
punished.

GIOVANNI: Oh sir, through your services our happiness is
restored. For this you will be richly rewarded.

GIOVANNI: O beloved daughter. Sir, I must go and see her.

ATTORNEY: You go ahead; I'll go to the Governor meanwhile.

DEMETRIO: I'll go with your lordship in case my help is needed.

ATTORNEY: An excellent idea.

SCENE IV   DEMETRIO, ATTORNEY, JORDANO

DEMETRIO: Look there sir. That's the Cavaliere Jordano, the one who tried to kill Gisippo and me a short time ago. If he attacks again, you'll be my witness that I am only defending myself.

ATTORNEY: But why should he want to kill you?

DEMETRIO: The Gisippo and Tindaro you've been hearing about are one and the same person. For this man and the Cavaliere, together with their two wives, destiny has fashioned a strange game which has brought us to these present circumstances. More of that at our leisure. Right now I must keep an eye on his every move.

JORDANO: Until I spill his blood, my rage will devour me. Here comes that friend of his — En garde!

ATTORNEY: What do you intend to do, Cavaliere?

JORDANO: Stand aside.

ATTORNEY: Why would you dare such insolence? Can't you see that I represent the Pope?

JORDANO: The Pope? What are you talking about?

ATTORNEY: Desist. What's your business with this man?

JORDANO: What business has Gisippo with my wife?

DEMETRIO: Only the business of an honest wedding. And what right have you to assault his wife and to hold her in bondage?

JORDANO: His wife?

DEMETRIO: Giulietta,

JORDANO: I know no Giulietta.

DEMETRIO: How about Agatina, then, the one you're trying
  to possess?

JORDANO: Agatina's not Gisippo's wife. She's one of
  Marabeo's slaves.

DEMETRIO: Nor does Gisippo know you as Madonna
  Argentina's husband.

JORDANO: But I am.

DEMETRIO: Possibly so, but nobody else knew it, least of all
  us.

ATTORNEY: Cavaliere, where men's lives are at stake, you
  cannot venture such brashness.

JORDANO: What gentleman would do otherwise whose
  honour has been violated, and whose wife has been
  compromised, in his own city, in his own house, and by
  a gang of cowardly foreigners?

DEMETRIO: You'd better keep your head, Cavaliere! Get
  this matter clear and start talking sense. We're not guilty
  of these crimes. To call us cowards is a brutal insult. We
  are foreigners, but we will show you that the Cortesi and
  Canali from Chios are families of dignity and substance
  and not to be abused with impunity.

JORDANO: It's getting better by the minute. First you want
  to deprive me of wife and possessions; now you'll strip
  me of both my family names.

DEMETRIO: What, are you a Cortesi?

JORDANO: Yes, if you please.

ATTORNEY: And a Canali?

JORDANO: My wife is, the one they're trying to take from
  me.

DEMETRIO: Who is your father?

JORDANO: What, you want to steal my father as well?

ATTORNEY: What old wive's tale is this? These two are about to become relatives of one another. Where is this Messer Gisippo?

DEMETRIO: In the house.

ATTORNEY: Have him come here, please.

SCENE V   ATTORNEY, GISIPPO, JORDANO, GIOVANNI, BATTISTA (scruffy scoundrels), PILUCCA, MARABEO

ATTORNEY: Cavaliere, if you behave so lightly and irresponsibly during the reign of this Pope, whatever head you have left will be chopped off. Your boldness has been excessive; you have created a private prison in the city of Rome, treated women brutally, attempted murder. Your behaviour shows nothing but contempt for so lofty a prince.

JORDANO: The revenge I seek is just. It is not punishment for my efforts I deserve, but compassion for my failure.

ATTORNEY: That's as you imagine it. But the reality is quite different.

JORDANO: Here comes that traitor, Gisippo.

ATTORNEY: Don't make a move, Cavaliere, until I get to the bottom of this. Approach, Messer Gisippo.

JORDANO: Gisippo! Gisippo!

GISIPPO: Jordano! Jordano!

ATTORNEY: No raging and shouting. Just answer my questions. Cavaliere, were you born in Rome?

JORDANO: I was born in Rome.

ATTORNEY: Is your father alive?

JORDANO: No sir.

ATTORNEY: And yours?

GISIPPO: Also deceased.

ATTORNEY: Where did yours come from?

JORDANO: Genoa.

ATTORNEY: And yours?

GISIPPO: Chios.

ATTORNEY: You both come from the same jurisdiction. Did their ancestors come from these places?

JORDANO: Mine used to say they were from Chios.

ATTORNEY: Now you're both from the same homeland.[72] Of which family is yours?

JORDANO: Cortesi.

ATTORNEY: And yours?

GISIPPO: Cortesi.

ATTORNEY: So, you're from the same family. What was your father's name?

GISIPPO: Messer Agapito.

ATTORNEY: And yours?

JORDANO: Messer Franco.

GISIPPO: You're the son of my uncle, Messer Franco?

JORDANO: And you of Messer Agapito my father's brother?

ATTORNEY: Take it easy.

JORDANO: I never heard he had a son called Gisippo.

GISIPPO: Tindaro perhaps?

JORDANO: Tindaro, yes. Are you Tindaro?

GISIPPO: I am.

JORDANO: But why Gisippo?

GISIPPO: For a good reason. Let it go at that.

ATTORNEY: Strange case. Clarify this doubt for me. Did you

83

know Gisippo, or Tindaro, whoever you are, that your father had a brother in Rome?

GISIPPO: No sir, I thought he was in Genoa.

ATTORNEY: Then, Cavaliere, your father came from Genoa to Rome?

JORDANO: He did sir, and opened a business here with the Centurioni four years before the sack of Rome,[73] and he died shortly before I was born.

ATTORNEY: This part is now clear. You're cousins beyond all doubt. But wait. You say, Cavaliere, that your lady is of the Canali family?

JORDANO: She is indeed.

ATTORNEY: Who was her father?

JORDANO: Messer Paolo Canali.

ATTORNEY: The one who was protonotary?[74]

JORDANO: The very one.

GISIPPO: What am I hearing? My Giulietta is Argentina's cousin!

ATTORNEY: How?

GISIPPO: This Messer Paolo was the brother of Giovanni Canali, the father of Giulietta, who is in Rome now with another brother.

ATTORNEY: And they are the scruffy scoundrels?

GISIPPO: That's what people call them. They belong to the Canali family.

JORDANO: Then these are my wife's uncles?

ATTORNEY: What a tangled affair this is.

JORDANO: I went to look for them in the East, and here they are in Rome.

ATTORNEY: What for?

JORDANO: To settle with them the inheritance from Messer Paolo's estate, which belongs to my wife.

ATTORNEY: This comes together perfectly, like cheese on macaroni. Now the transaction can be completed. But Tindaro, Jordano, why do you continue to scowl? Don't you recognize one another? You're brothers.

GISIPPO: Cavaliere, words cannot express my emotions. My soul tells me that you are of my own blood, and that I must forgive your transgressions and receive you as a brother.

JORDANO: Likewise, I want to pardon you for your offenses, but such insults to my honour rankle in my breast.

GISIPPO: Rather in attempting my Giulietta by force, you have violated my honour.

JORDANO: I had no way of knowing that she was Giulietta or that she was yours. And what's more, though I tried, I had no success.

GISIPPO: Nor did I intend you any dishonour. The marriage negotiations between Madonna Argentina and myself were proper in every way, since you were thought dead, and we were both unaware of the family ties between us. Now you're alive and the wedding did not take place. What then is her offense or mine?

JORDANO: I suspect adultery.

ATTORNEY: Ah, Cavaliere, on the part of Madonna Argentina?

GISIPPO: There is no shred of evidence even to suggest it. It is I who should suspect it of you, since my lady was fully in your power.

JORDANO: You may be proud of her, Tindaro; she's a lady of incontestable virtue and constancy. She submitted to no violation at my hand.

GISIPPO: As I accept your word, so you, as my brother, must accept mine: your lady remains totally free of taint.

JORDANO: I'm inclined to believe you. Your words and the record of her past life convince me that she is as chaste as ever. I accept you as my dear cousin.

ATTORNEY: Just see how much harmony has been born out of such confusion. I swear, it's a veritable comedy. And here come the scruffy brothers decked out in new attire.

GIOVANNI: Scruffy we were, but now we've abandoned our rags.

BATTISTA: We're rich.

GIOVANNI: We're elated.

BATTISTA: Our lunacy is over.

GIOVANNI: Today we've gained three hundred thousand ducats.

BATTISTA: And rediscovered our lost daughter.

GISIPPO: And you've acquired a son, namely me.

JORDANO: And found a niece, who is my wife.

GIOVANNI: Niece? What niece? Now that we're rich, the relatives start flocking around.

BATTISTA: Niece on the money's side.

ATTORNEY: Niece on the side of your own blood, daughter of your brother Messer Paolo.

GIOVANNI: Of Messer Paolo, our brother?

BATTISTA: Of Messer Paolo?

ATTORNEY: Ah, here she is. And here is Messer Demetrio and Giulietta. If we have to wait for everyone to welcome everyone else and give a speech, we'll be here all night. Hold off, my friends. I'll give you a nice medley of everything: Cavaliere, Madonna Argentina is your wife and an honourable lady. To her you owe love and honour. Tindaro and Giulietta are husband and wife by mutual consent. Gentlemen, to them you owe your blessings.

GIOVANNI: We are pleased to welcome him into the family, and we wish to offer him one hundred thousand ducats of our earnings as a dowry.

ATTORNEY: Very tidy!

GIOVANNI: And to you for your industry and concern, two thousand.

ATTORNEY: I'm indebted to you for your courtesy and generosity. You should also take into consideration that Madonna Argentina, wife of the Cavaliere here, is the daughter of Messer Paolo Canale, your brother. This makes her your niece, Giulietta's cousin and Tindaro's sister-in-law; Tindaro is, by the same token, Madonna Argentina's brother-in-law and Jordano's cousin; Jordano is Tindaro's cousin and Giulietta's brother-in-law; Giulietta is Jordano's sister-in-law and cousin to Argentina. And you are the fathers, uncles and fathers-in-law of Giulietta, Argentina, Jordano and Tindaro. Where there is union, let it be strengthened; where no union is possible, let love turn into charity. Now, share the embrace all around. At your leisure you can speak the sweet words that are in your hearts.

PILUCCA: Here's a whole lot of hugging and squeezing, Marabeo. Come out here, things may be looking up for us too.

MARABEO: Do you see the Captain of the Guards anywhere?

PILUCCA: He's not here. Come on out.

MARABEO: Have a good look.

ATTORNEY: Aha! Here are the thieves. We need only to see you hanged to make our rejoicing complete. I'm going to the Governor to arrange this service for you.

JORDANO: But sir, since I'm involved in their crimes, such an order would destroy my peace. Let us not sully so festive an occasion. As a favour to me I ask you not to carry charges against them.

ATTORNEY: All right — but it won't be long before the gallows catch up with them anyway.

PILUCCA: No, listen. From now on we promise to be good and honest men.

ATTORNEY: It won't be easy for you two.

MARABEO: Allow us to beg forgiveness of Madonna Giulietta.

ATTORNEY: By all means, and make sure that none of these previous affairs is seen or heard of again.

MARABEO: Does that include my account books? That would be a blessing, by God.

PILUCCA: Well then, isn't your Master's return gain enough?

MARABEO: How very true. I'm happy as things are. I wouldn't want the Cavaliere to be troubled with the accounts. Master, let's agree that they are settled between us. Anything you still owe me, I'll willingly forego as a gift to you.

ATTORNEY: When these thieves should be making restitution they demand even more! It's just like in the days of Ciollo the Abbot.[75]

JORDANO: I too am satisfied. Come then, let's celebrate.

ATTORNEY: Let happiness be yours all around, now and forever. Strike up the wedding festivities and be you merrymakers all. And you, gentle spectators, present us with signs of joyfulness.

Notes

1. *Avino-Avolio* — two of the knights errant (paladins) at the court of Charlemagne; in Ariosto's *Orlando Furioso* they are inseparable companions.

2. *Castor and Pollux* — in Greek mythology they figure among the *Dioscuri* or sons of Zeus. Their mother was Leda. Tales associated with them deal largely with their bravery and military exploits. They were later adopted by the Romans who built a temple to them in their capital. When Castor was killed, Pollux, who was immortal, asked permission to die so that he could share his immortality with his beloved brother. Jupiter (Zeus) allowed them to spend alternating days in heaven and hades.

3. *Farnese family* — one of the most powerful of Italian aristocratic families during the Renaissance. Caro had been employed by Pierluigi Farnese just a few months before writing this comedy. Pierluigi was the son of Pope Paul III (Alessandro Farnese) whose greatness as prince and prelate is several times mentioned in the play. Paul III was, indeed, one of the most outstanding of the Renaissance Popes and his death in 1549 brought about general mourning. If he had a weakness it was in his favouritism to family members, including Pierluigi, to whom he gave the rule of Piacenza and Parma, an investiture so badly handled that it led to Pierluigi's assassination by irate citizens. He was a man of the lowest moral character whom Burckhardt called "terrible," and who was a prime target of Aretino's satire during his lifetime.

4. *scudi* — name still used for large silver coins. It took the name from the fact that when first introduced the coins showed the escutcheon of the prince or of the issuing nation on one of its faces. At the beginning they were made of gold, and were known as scudi of the sun because they had a small sun at the beginning of the inscription. The coin was imported into Italy from France in the sixteenth century, and it soon replaced the ducat even in those states where the ducat had first been minted — Venice and Florence. When an equivalent silver coin was minted, it replaced the gold ones and soon *scudo* became the denomination of all other silver coins.

5. *Grimaldi* — a wealthy family from Genoa. The litigation between the two brothers Giovanni and Battista and the Grimaldi constitutes one of the main threads of the plot.

6. *a feast of hot air* — literally "like a chap who paid hard cash for feasting only on the smoke of roasting meat," a reference to the ninth tale of the thirteenth-century collection of short stories known as *Il Novellino*, in which the Saracen cook Fabrac demands to be paid by a poor man for having allowed him to dip a piece of bread in the smoke coming from one of the pots on the stove.

7. *ghostly characters* — Giovanni and Battista.

8. *in three ways* — Renaissance comedy, imitating the Latin, had to be simple in action like the original model. Yet, under the influence of Boccaccio's *Decameron*, the plot had become more complex. In the case of Caro's play the plot develops into three actions, as is explained just after.

9. a metaphor based on the Renaissance theory of the humours and of digestion.

10. *Ripa* — a quarter in the city of Rome.

11. *Ponte* — The bridge leading to Castel Sant'Angelo.

12. *Farnese Palace* — a palace designed by Antonio da Sangallo (d. 1546) as a modest town house for Cardinal Alessandro Farnese who, when he was elevated to Pope, had it converted into a grand residence ostensibly for himself, but actually for Caro's patron Pierluigi, his illegitimate son. Construction continued until 1550 and included contributions by Michelangelo.

13. *Greco* — a street in Rome, but also a reference to the white wine called "greco."

14. *Corso* — mentioned not only to elaborate on the joke about wine, this time alluding to a white wine from Corsica, but also to call attention to the grand renovation projects carried out during the pontificate of Pope Paul III. Streets were drained, leveled and widened, new public squares were created, slum houses were replaced, all under the direction of the *maestro delle strade*, Latino Manetti. At this time Corso was turned into a magnificent boulevard, one of the finest in Rome. Much of the work took place during the years of Pilucca's absence; hence his confusion.

15. *Mazzacane* — probably another reference to a wine from the region of Campania.

16. *Campo di Fiori* — a square in the centre of Rome and in one

90

of the most populous areas of the city very close to the Pantheon.

17. *Barbagrigia* — the famous editor and printer Antonio Blado d'Asola, friend of Caro and co-member of the semi-serious Academy of Virtue.

18. *scrawny* — in the original Barbagrigia makes a pun on the name Pilucca and the verb *piluccare*, to nibble away.

19. *Moors* — the fear of Turks was a real one, yet by Caro's time it had also become a common literary *topos*.

20. *bloody rod and magic thread* — the ruddle and the plumb-line of Boccaccio, an otherwise unidentifiable person who represents the foreman of a demolition and construction company.

21. *a work of such splendour* — the new Farnese palace.

22. the island of Chios, which at the time belonged to Genoa.

23. *the nuns of Genoa* — Bandello, *Novelle I, 53:* "At present I want to do just as Uncle Pedrone told me several times the nuns of Genoa do, for they go wherever they feel like within the town and even outside, and when they return to the convent they tell their Mother Superior: 'Mother, with your permission we went for a little recreation, to take an airing'."

24. *Turkish vessels* — light and fast pirate boats with one mast and two or three guns.

25. *Cephalonia* — Zacintus and Cephalonia, islands off the west coast of Greece, were both in the possession of Venice, important links in their eastern trade route. At the time of the writing of the play the sea power of Venice was decidedly on the wane. She was never to recover from the crippling effect of the League of Cambrai of 1508, when the major powers of Europe united to strip her of her powers on land and sea. From that time onwards, the Ottomans carried out attack after attack against Venice's eastern possessions. In 1535 she lost Egina, Paros and Syra, in 1540 Malvasia and Nauplia. These were the years just before and during the time Pilucca was made a slave in the Turkish galleys. 1532 was a turning point since in this year Sulieman failed in his second attempt on the city of Vienna and thus turned all his efforts against Italy and the islands in the Mediterranean. The Emperor Charles V carried out a successful Tunisian campaign against Muslim pirates in 1535, but the effects were short lived. By the time of his last attack against the Corsairs in 1541 the Turks were in virtual control. Pilucca's plight was a common one. After a united western victory against the Turks in the famous sea battle of

Lepanto in 1571 some 15,000 Christian slaves were set at liberty.

26. *down to the last cent* — literally "down to the fennel," meaning at that time the last dish in a meal.

27. *just like the Scriptures said* — Psalm CXIII: "Mare vidit et fugit, Jordanis conversus est retrosum." Marabeo's pun is on the name Giordano, the husband of Argentina, and the river Jordan of the Psalm.

28. *Pleuripathetics and Stoiters* — comic deformation of Peripatetics and Stoics, two ancient schools of philosophy.

29. *alphabastards* — in the original *Alfabecochi*, a word made up of *alfa* — the first letter of the Greek alphabet — and *becchi* — cuckolds.

30. *a dirty old man* — in the original "one of the dirty old men of Susan," i.e. one of the elders who had peeped at Susanna while she was bathing. The story is told in the apocryphal portion of the Book of Daniel, Chap. XIII.

31. *the egg of the Ascension* — on Ascension day it was customary in Rome to place an egg at the window to keep evil away. Proverbially someone who could not be saved even by the egg of the Ascension was one condemned to die.

32. *plaster* — during the Renaissance, plasters were made of wine and spices and applied to the injured part with wet cloths.

33. The name Argentina derives from *argento*, silver, hence Barbagrigia's *double entendre*.

34. *nitwit* — in the original "Giutta," who is the traditional figure of the idiot.

35. *Master Gisippo's misery* — the fact that he was forced to marry against his will in order to please his friend and that he was hoping for an early death in order to rejoin his beloved in heaven.

36. *Pussy-cat* — in Italian *gattina*, little cat, an obvious pun on the name of the girl, Agatina.

37. The original sentence is based on military terms.

38. Literally "make sure the devil doesn't get into the basin."

39. *gilé* — a card game popular at the time.

40. *julians* — Papal coins minted under Pope Julius II as an improved and more valuable version of the Papal carlin. The name *giulio* was kept until the Pontificate of Pope Paul III when it took the name *paolo*.

41. *Mamelukes* — name of the famous Turkish warriors who seized Egypt in 1254. In Arabic the word meant "slave" and in Europe became synonymous with frightening beings, devils.

42. *the Great Turk* — the name given in the west to the Sultan of the Turkish Empire.

43. The comic device of the hyperbolic non-existent number derives from the *Decameron*: VI.10 and VIII.3.

44. *Monte Mario* — a quarter in Rome, at that time outside the city walls.

45. *Janissaries* — the select guard of the Sultans. They had a reputation for being thiefs and ravagers, hence the following pun about their being in the pontifical chancellery.

46. *Testaccio* — one of the poorest quarters in Rome.

47. *Trebisonda* — a city on the south east shore of the Black Sea, an important seat of government in the Byzantine Empire until its fall to the Turks in 1461 eight years after the fall of Constantinople. Here the use of the name has a comic effect (see also Aretino, *Astrologo* 1,2.).

48. *mitre* — the *mitra* was the Papal cap, but it was also the name of the cap given to those put in the pillory.

49. A reference to the shameful torture of being beaten with a broom.

50. *Picardy* — traditionally it was the region of the *impiccati*, of those who had been hanged. To send someone to Picardy meant to have someone hanged (see Ariosto's *Negromante*, V. 6). Mirandola in fact will be given, as a symbol of his investiture, the halter.

51. *the Count of Hangland* — in Italian the *Count of Boiona*, i.e. the *boia*, the hangman.

52. The necklace is the hanging rope and the sentence means that if the necklace will cause Mirandola to die by hanging, he will never die of hunger.

53. *tif taf* — voices in imitation of drums and trumpets, mocking a military parade.

54. *planted the carrot in him* — made him suspicious.

55. Pilucca understands the previous remark as meaning that Argentina is a woman of loose morals.

56. *it's his tough luck* — the original uses the proverbial expression *fare il becco all'oca*, i.e. to complete the business.

57. *our lawyer* — Messer Rossello.

58. literally, "the thirty pair of devils got loose today."

59. *a warrant* — in the original "a warrant *de capiendo*."

60. The original has a pun on the word *incoronazione* (coronation) and the misspelling of it by Mirandola, whose *incoronazione* comes to mean cuckolding.

61. *Caliph Timer Lung* — (fl. 1336-1405), known as Tamburlaine to the English-speaking world, was a Mongol warrior whose invasion of India was famed for its ruthlessness. There are comic intentions both in the spelling of the name in the play and in mistaking him for a Caliph — a Muslim title.

62. *Bucephallus* — the horse of Alexander the Great, here intentionally misspelled for comic effect in order to parallel a pun in the original text.

63. *Salah-ed-din* — Saladin, the legendary Sultan of Egypt who lived in the thirteenth century.

64. *the Empress of Orbec* — probably a comic reference to Giambattista Giraldi Cinzio's tragedy *Orbecche*, staged in 1541 and printed in 1543.

65. *the eyes of the dragon* — the two brothers had lent money to the Grimaldi for the statue of St. George slaying the dragon.

66. *Tobias* — the *Book of Tobias* (V-VII) relates the story of Tobias' journey to the Medes to collect a debt, accompanied by the angel Raphael.

67. *Tarquinius* — Sextus Tarquinius, son of the King of Rome Tarquinius Superbus, who possessed Lucretia, the wife of Tarquinius Collatinus, by threatening her with a dagger.

68. *the bloodstone of Calandrino* — the stone that renders those who possess it invisible. The story of Calandrino is in the *Decameron* VIII.3.

69. *the ring of Angelica* — the ring that made the heroine of Ariosto's *Orlando Furioso* invisible (X.4; XII.4; XXIX.64).

70. While the middle and the end of Giulietta's letter seem original with Caro, the beginning translates almost word for word Leucippe's letter to Cleitophon in Achilles Tatius' *Leucippe and Cleitophon*, a Greek romance written at the end of the third century A.D. and well known to Caro. The beginning of Leucippe's letter reads: "Lord I must call you, as you are my lady's husband. You know what I have suffered for your sake, but perforce I must remind you of it." Title translated in the Loeb Classical Library as *The Adventures of Leucippe and Clitophon*, trans. S. Gaselee (Boston, 1961), Bk V, 18, p. 277.

71. Even this passage, which because of its contrasts (*I burn, I tremble*, etc.) points to a Petrarchan model, comes directly from Tatius, loc. cit.: "At this message I was moved with many emotions at once; I was flushed and pale, I was astonished and incredulous, I was full of joy and sorrow." "Do you come bringing this letter from Hades?" I said to Satyrus, "or what does this mean? Has Leucippe come to life again?" See also our introduction.

72. *You both come from the same jurisdiction* — see note 22.

73. *before the sack of Rome* — in 1523 an army of German mercenaries, joined by the forces of Charles Duke of Milan, ransacked Rome.

74. *protonotary* — the chief clerk in the law courts.

75. *the days of Ciollo the Abbot* — a proverbial expression, possibly deriving from Dante's reference to Ciolo degli Abati in his *Epistola* IX (to his Florentine friend) as an example of an infamous individual who was nevertheless forgiven and allowed to return from banishment to the city of Florence.